EFT is Simple. People are Complex.

Praise for *EFT is Simple. People are Complex.*

Quite simply, Ann Adams is one of the best teachers I know. I don't just mean that she is a great tapping instructor, but she is an amazing teacher of the human condition. As the title *EFT is Simple; People are Complex* denotes, the tapping part is the easy part. It is understanding the human part that is hard. Ann does an amazing job in this book, in simple bite-size easy to understand chunks, laying out a path to not only understanding what it means to be human but how to use tapping to improve the quality of this experience. If you are new to tapping, this book is a must-have as it is an amazing introduction to so many useful concepts in an easily approachable way. If you are an experienced tapper, you are going to get more out of your tapping practice though the subtleties and nuances that Ann provides. This is a must-own, and more importantly, a must-read for anyone interested in getting more out of their tapping practice.

Gene Monterastelli, TappingQandA.com

Ann Adam's newest book, *EFT is Simple; People are Complex*, is simply a must-have for your personal growth bookshelf. There are few people in the EFT Tapping field that I have such respect for. Her decades of experience as a practitioner, trainer, teacher of trainers, and developer of EFT teaching methods puts her in a class of her own. This book feels like the culmination of all of her experience compiled in an easy-to-read and perfectly organized manner. Her examples and metaphors and flow charts are clearly the distillation of a lifetime of study and practice.

As a trainer myself I found myself soaking up her wisdom, learning new ways to explain concepts, and greatly appreciated her willingness to offer both structure and flexibility in her approaches. I highly recommend this to anyone who is looking for well-organized, well-written, and technically acurate easy-to-read book that takes a deep dive into understanding so many applications of EFT.

Craig Weiner, DC,
EFT Tapping Training Institute Director,
EFT International Master Trainer of Trainers

Ann displays an impressive combination of care and professionalism, a combination that serves in the highest way for both clients and practitioners. She embraces recognizing the client and where they are with compassion, knowledge, and training. I have always admired Ann's combination of deep care while also bringing great intelligence and knowledge to all she does. No matter whether you are an EFT newby or a seasoned professional, this book has something for everyone. I will be recommending it to my practitioners as well as clients.

Maggie Adkins, EFT Founding Master, TBT (Trauma Buster Technique) Practitioner

I attended Ann's first EFT workshop in 2000 and have been using EFT with clients ever since. *EFT is Simple – People are Complex* covers a variety of topics, giving suggestions and examples of approaches to using EFT. It is a worthwhile read for beginners and experienced practitioners as well. I enjoyed reading it and, even after 20 years of using EFT, I gained additional ideas for dealing with challenging situations.

Cheryl Melton, LMFT, EFT Practitioner

I have always appreciated Ann's spirit, calm and grounded, a no non-sense yet non-judgmental direct approach. And very generous. Also, the quiet, and deep reverence for humanity, and respect for children, especially the ones who are going through or have survived tremendous suffering. I became a big fan and an avid reader of Ann's blogs. This compilation of the reader's favorites is a wonderful companion and useful follow up to EFT training. *EFT is Simple – People are Complex* is a place to receive silent mentoring any time of the day and to gain insight into this rich field. We now have an opportunity to directly absorb her pragmatic, yet organic and humanistic, approach to better understanding of EFT, business practice tips, even life guidance from a wisdom holder, all in one handy book. A must read for anyone interested in and loving EFT!

Mitsuko Ito, Advanced EFT Practitioner

Ann Adams, who I often refer to as "the original EFT Master," shares her years of successful EFT experiences in an extremely useful collection, *EFT is Simple – People Are Complex*. In my own professional journey, I see the beauty and wisdom of that title. I have always appreciated Ann's clarity, practicality, and honesty that run throughout all her work, training, and interviews. Just as importantly, I have valued her emphasis upon compassionate respect for the human condition, especially in working with children.

The lifetime of experiential wisdom in this work has been thoughtfully edited and efficiently paced to serve busy modern day health & wellness professionals achieve excellent, satisfying results from this caretaking work we've chosen to do in an ever-more complex world. For that reason, I can honestly say that we all need to add this book to our healing and helping toolboxes. Although the book is geared toward our work with clients, readers will find it equally useful when doing peer-to-peer and self-care.

Jondi Whitis, EFT International MTOT

Ann Adams uses her many years of experience to pull together and cement information useful for all EFT practitioners and expands on any EFT class. This book is an important learning support covering many topics often brought up in a mentoring session after training. This book is well worth studying to increase your understanding of important concepts behind every successful EFT session.

Emma Roberts, EFT Founding Master,
EFT International MTOT

This collection of articles is full of clear wisdom and practical knowhow to help you bridge the gap between the power and the simplicity of EFT with the varied complexity of each individual. Read these short pieces over and over and each time gain a new insight or understanding to help you better help yourself and others with EFT.

Gwyneth Moss, EFT Founding Master,
EFT International MTOT

Just like my experiences learning from Ann in-person, this book is about so much more than studying EFT. Her words are timeless reminders of what actually matters in the helping professions—have respect, show compassion, be effective—not only to others but especially to yourself. As someone fairly new to EFT, this book is truly a treasure.

Rachel Newman, MA, CHHP

EFT is Simple. People are Complex. by Ann Adams

Copyright © 2021 Ann Adams.

ISBN: 9781736684504

Published by Ann Adams, EFT Master Training

www.annadams.com

All rights reserved. This book and any portions thereof may not be reproduced in any form whatsoever without written permission from the author. For reproduction requests contact ann@annadams.com

Edited by Dominique Monette, Emma Roberts, and Jondi Whitis

Printed in the United States of America.

EFT IS SIMPLE
PEOPLE ARE COMPLEX

*Safely & Effectively Navigating
the Complexities with
Emotional Freedom Techniques*

ANN ADAMS

Dedicated with deep gratitude for all those people throughout my life who believed in me, supported me, and encouraged me, whether simply a kind word from a stranger on a bad day, or the people who always seemed to be there when I needed them. Thank you.

To my daughter who will always live in my heart.

And to "Lulu" who still patiently sits here :-)

Table of Contents

Preface	13
1 | Ready, Willing, and Able	17
2 | Working In The Dark	23
3 | Introducing EFT to Your Clients	29
4 | How Does EFT Work?	33
5 | Your Space Reflects Your Values	35
6 | Upside and Downside of Being Real	39
7 | What is the Purpose of Sneaking Up?	45
8 | Missed Opportunities	49
9 | Does One Size Ever Fit All?	53
10 | EFT Shortcut – Ace-in-the-Hole	57
11 | Assessing Intensity and Clarity	61
12 | When Amy Gets Upset	67
13 | How Veterans Perceive Therapy and Therapists	73
14 | Constricted Breathing	77
15 | Changing Addictive Behavior	83
16 | Individualizing Affirmations	87
17 | EFT and Dreams	91
18 | How Do Innovations Spread?	95
19 | EFT is Like Systematic Desensitization	101
20 | Simple and Complex Phobias	105
21 | Muscle Testing	109
22 | Experiencing Grief	113
23 | Tapping Does the Work	117
24 | Too Much Too Soon	121
25 | Pros and Cons of Intakes	127

26 | Being vs. Doing	131
27 | In Defense of Resistance	135
28 | Is Reframing Necessary?	143
29 | How to Create Reframes	147
30 | The Beginning of Research into Energy Psychology	153
31 | How Gary Craig Got into the VA	157
32 | It Worked!! It Worked!! It Worked!!	161
33 | Pendulums and Jugs	163
34 | *The* Problem vs. *My* Problem	167
35 | Are You as Good as You Could Be?	169
36 | EFT and NLP	173
37 | Guidelines for Thought Disorders	179
38 | Trivia – the eft	183
39 | Another Bridge to EFT	185
40 | Support for Practitioners	189
41 | Self-Care Practices	193
42 | Daily Tapping Routine	197
43 | Using Pre-sleep Moments	201
44 | What is Your Talisman?	203
45 | Hardwiring Happiness	207
46 | Motivating Literature	209
APPENDIX 1 | EFT Level 1 and 2 Training Review	217
ADDITIONAL OPTIONS FOR TAPPING	243
APPENDIX 2 | In Pursuit of Excellence	249
About The Author	275

Preface

Curiosity led me to attend my first Introductory EFT class at an NASW-GA (National Association for Social Work-Georgia) Conference in 1999. Fascination led me to seek additional information and training. Skepticism gave way to awe. Hundreds of clients and students later, I remain in awe of the power of EFT and its impact on my life and the life of my EFT students and clients. Now a *retired* licensed clinical social worker, I've been working with people in various roles for over 40 years in the mental health field for the last twenty years, including implementing, teaching, and writing about EFT.

This book offers support and knowledge for anyone exploring EFT. It offers reminders of, and ways to deal with, the complexity of human beings, and hopefully increases your ability to see people, situations, and application of EFT in even more effective ways. It shares ways you can implement this powerful skill into other techniques or modalities you already use with your clients. It is simple to modify EFT to fit your approaches and your client to improve results.

This is not a textbook on EFT, nor a complete study of the complexity of people. It shares ideas to better focus on the person sitting in front of you as a unique human being. Because we learn best from stories, many of the articles give real-life examples. However, all details are modified to prevent the recognition of any person or their story.

If you have not had formal training in EFT, or it's been a while since you attended, you may wish to begin by reading Appendix I, EFT Level 1 and 2 Review.

Years ago, during an interview on an EFT radio show. I made the statement that while the steps of EFT are relatively simple, individual people can be very complex. It was one of those common sense "reframes" in perception concerning something we already "knew" but often never perceived it in that way before. This statement resonated with many as I received multiple positive emails and phone calls.

Those responses led to four years' worth of almost weekly emails with short articles in which I attempted to point out the complexities of people and their problems and to share useful ways to deal with those complexities and individual differences in reactions. At times I also shared or expanded upon useful ideas from other practitioners. This book is the result of encouragement from students and newsletter readers to pull the posts together in a book. It is a compilation, and major re-edit, of the best of my readers' favorites *and* a few new ones.

In my journey in the energy psychology world, I attended thirteen of Gary Craig's early weekend workshops and many other related energy classes with certifications and titles. I am now retired from them all. The ones I am most proud of are the EFT certifications. The EFT-Cert-Honors from Gary Craig, the founder of EFT, and working with Gary Craig on several projects, including being the Director of his EFT Master Program, and helping to establish EFT training guidelines. Gary no longer sponsors either program as he has moved on to other projects. However, those EFT training guidelines still form the basis for EFT training and accrediting bodies around the world.

I held the Master Trainer of Trainers title from EFT International (formerly known as the Association for the Advancement of Meridian Energy Therapies or AAMET); ACP-EFT certification with Tina Craig through ACEP (Association for Comprehensive Energy Psychology), and as a DCEP consultant with ACEP.

I've written chapters for EFT books and co-authored *EFT Level*

PREFACE

1 (2 and 3) Comprehensive Training Resource. I created *EFT4Power-Point*, a "workshop in a box" for those wishing to share EFT with others. This program was recommended by Gary when he did have guidelines for training and has sold over 2000 copies, literally over the world.

The last twenty years have been delightful, fascinating, and challenging, full of numerous experiences that broadened and added to my life. I met and continue to meet so many wonderful people. The people and experiences I've met along the way and the memories I continue to carry are treasured far above any title or certification. I owe much to EFT and to people too numerous to name. They and EFT changed my life. Perhaps even saved my life. A few years ago, I was very ill. Jondi Whitis organized EFTers around the world to tap for my "very best outcome." If you were one of those people—Thank you! I was and am very grateful.

This book is *not* a how-to-do EFT book; it's a book full of ideas, suggestions, and examples of using EFT even more successfully. Some of which I've learned the hard way! This book is not just about my hard-earned wisdom in working with people; it is about life. I hope that in some small way, this book adds to your life and your EFT journey.

Warmly,

Ann

1

Ready, Willing, and Able

> **IN A NUTSHELL:** Clients vary in their abilities, needs, and expectations. Our approaches need to vary as well. Clients come to us in various stages of readiness, willingness, and ability to fully benefit from their sessions. Indeed, a key purpose of an initial assessment—whatever format is used, or information requested—is to assess *how* ready, willing, and able the client is to participate. This information enables us to create an individualized approach that will be most helpful to that client at that time. Each client comes in with individual expectations. Assessing expectations that the client brings to the session also impacts how we address each client.

Roshane lost trust in her practitioner and stopped sessions. She felt the practitioner attempted to do "too much too fast" and felt the practitioner "was pushing her agenda." Roshane indicated she needed, and wanted, more time to process and talk about the issue. She was "uncomfortable" with the way the practitioner "pushed" her to find a specific event and begin tapping sooner than she felt ready.

Two Sides to Every Story

- Perhaps the practitioner did not pre-frame what would

happen in the session, and Roshane did not ask.

- Perhaps the practitioner did pre-frame and attempted to clarify what Roshane wanted and expected from the EFT session, and Roshane agreed but gave no feedback. After all, clients—and ourselves—often act from unconscious motivations. *We don't always know what we want or perhaps are not comfortable giving feedback to the "expert."*

- Perhaps Roshane's belief was that if someone really cared about her, he or she would just "know" what she needed/wanted.

- Perhaps the practitioner thought she should indeed "know" and acted on her assumptions to the detriment of the client and herself.

- Perhaps Roshane took an immediate dislike to the practitioner, for who knows what reason, and nothing the practitioner did would have been "right."

- Perhaps the practitioner was inexperienced and felt she had to find a specific event and start tapping right away, more focused on getting results than attuning to the client.

- Perhaps she hadn't established sufficient rapport and/or gathered sufficient background information.

- Perhaps Roshane is a very angry person who is only able to feel good about herself if she criticizes someone else, and the practitioner was in the wrong place at the wrong time.
- Perhaps the practitioner was aware of Roshane's reluctance, but felt tapping would resolve her discomfort.
- Perhaps Roshane was unable to say to the practitioner what she wanted and needed.
- Perhaps she was an expert at hiding what she felt and wanted, taught as a young child not to share what she wanted, that her role in life was going along, not to confront, not to ask.

Perhaps a lot of things.

Whatever occurred, the result was Roshane's expectations were not met as to what she wanted to, or thought should, happen. She was not "ready" to move so quickly. She was not "willing" to go at a fast pace. She was not "able" to process feelings and the changes, at least not at the pace she believed the practitioner wanted. Whatever happened, or for whatever reason, the practitioner missed Roshane's "ready, willing and able" signs for *what* to address, *how* it was addressed, *and the timing* used for addressing it.

Everyone has their own path, their own timing, and their own journey.*

Our challenge is to discover that path, timing, and journey and, with the client's permission, walk it with them. We can only hope to be the right person, with the right tool, applied in the right way, at the right time, in the right place. We are responsible *to* our client for being fully present, to listen closely, and for continuing to develop our skills and abilities.

We are *not* responsible *for* the client—and cannot be.

Consciously or unconsciously, most of us recognize the necessity to clarify some level of client needs and expectations. There are many different questions we could ask to begin gaining information and gently discover how "ready, willing, and able" (RWA) they are to work on their issues, right now.

Practitioners most often ask direct questions to assess RWA both at the beginning of each session and at times during sessions. The challenge with direct questions, especially initially, is that initial answers are *not* always a true representation of the issue.

> **Trust is a time thing.***

Rapport may happen quickly, but real trust and feeling safe takes time. Some clients are only willing to dip their toe in to test the water, so to speak. Their first answer is not always the real—or at least the main—answer. Indeed, your client may honestly not know.

Let's look at utilizing a more *indirect* approach to assessing RWA and building an environment of safety.

READY

Typical Direct Question: "How ready are you to resolve this issue?" Again, your client may not know. Most often there is a conflict involved. They may say they are ready but have little or no idea of the unconscious resistance or part of themselves that is nowhere near ready.

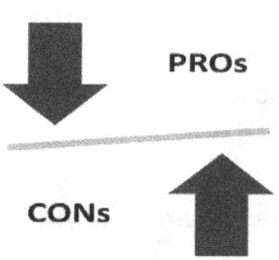

I've heard therapists talk about "resistant" clients as if this were a rare phenomenon. Let me strongly challenge that. Given the timing and issue, we can all become resistant.

We all have some level of conflict about changing. Significant others, family, friends, community, may impact the person's actual willingness and ability to change. Indeed, if there were not some conflict about changing, the necessary change would have already occurred; they would not be there with you.

Try a less direct approach starting with:

"**There are pros and cons to every change. What do you think might get in the way of your resolving this?**" This is a great question for assessing readiness and ability and beginning the process of dealing with the conflict. You gain a front-row seat to their level of awareness.

WILLING

Typical Direct Question: "What changes are you willing to make in your life now?" This can be a useful question for *bringing up resistance*, especially early when working on an issue.

A better question to allow you to address challenges to change would be:

"**As you think about making changes around this issue what comes up for you?**"

ABLE

Typical Direct Question: "How comfortable are you in talking about this right now?" The answer may allow you to begin tapping around their physical discomfort. The challenge is that tapping *right away* may bring up "too much too soon."

Ask this one first.

"**How do you generally calm yourself when you are upset?**" Their answers give you more background and a better idea of the client's skills in self-regulating their emotions. This question can guide how fast and direct you can go. Watch for how they respond to you and how they describe responding to others and the world.

Fragile clients often have learned to protect themselves by putting on a "face" to the world that they are OK. You've heard the expression not to take things at "face value." The client may present with sufficient ego strength and ability to "self-regulate," i.e., their ability to calm and control their emotions, or at least the emotions they present at the time. They may *not* realistically be as strong as they first appear. These clients need a slower pace and fewer direct questions. We all have our fragile parts. We can all join the "resistant" category around certain issues or parts of an issue in our life. It is safer, and more respectful, to err on the side of gentleness.

> **If you think someone has it all together you just don't know them well enough.***

Try beginning the tapping portion of your session with a focus on the breath. Our emotions often show up in our level of breathing. Not only is it a great way to introduce EFT, but it is also a great way to begin the calming process no matter the presenting issue. Focusing on the breath is especially useful for new clients and those with chronically high levels of anxiety, and an easy to learn self-help skill. Tapping for the percent of a full breath helps evaluate their level of body awareness and how able they are to respond to EFT and to address the issues. Teaching the client to focus on their breath helps increases self-use and eliminates the confusion frequently felt as to *how* they would address which issue and *what* to say as they tap.

How ready, willing, or able your client will influence how fast or slow, how directly or indirectly you need to address the issues, and whether to ask or not ask questions. The less ready, willing, and able the client is translates to spending more time getting to know your client, developing rapport, building trust, building a sense of safety, and sneaking up on the issues.

NOTES

Credits
Photo by Christina @ wocintechchat.com on Unsplash.com modified for EFT4PowerPoint
V3020
*An Annism

2

Working In The Dark

IN A NUTSHELL: When the client is reluctant to share what is upsetting them, EFT can still be used to address the physical reaction to the situation. "Working in the dark" with EFT gives respect for their privacy, and you are still able to teach a new skill to deal effectively with their emotions.

George, like many of the adolescents in his unit, did not want to talk about his past. Many residents are triggered by actions or behaviors they interpret as similar to a previous negative, sometimes horrendous experience. Small for his age, George had been badly abused by his older brothers when they were on drugs and often picked on by the other children in his previous foster and school settings.

He was very sensitive to any comment that could, in any way, be interpreted as negative towards him. It didn't take much. His experience was one of being taken advantage of, and hurt by, the very people who should have been supportive and protective. He had a hard time trusting people, and, like so many of the residents of the treatment center, had good reasons to feel as he did.

While we worked hard to help kids like George learn to process their feelings with their therapist or primary staff, developing that skill was difficult for many of the children we served, and, due to their previous experience, often took a long time. When I came to the unit, George was clearly upset, gone into his room, refused to participate in other unit activities, and refused to talk to staff. Fortunately, with EFT, it is not necessary to talk about the problem to use EFT effectively. We could "work in the dark."

Build a Bridge – Depending on the age, developmental stage, and earlier awareness of EFT, I give a short explanation along the lines of *I have an unusual way to relax that helps people feel better. I use it myself when I have something that upsets me and want to calm down quickly so I can think better about what to do. You don't have to talk about the problem or the bad feeling either for this to help. You can talk about it later if you want to—or not. Would you like to try it with me?*

I varied my approach depending on my knowledge of the resident, our depth of rapport, the level of obvious upset. I may encourage them to focus on what they are feeling in their body as we tap, using either no words or only a few words, e.g., really upset, really mad. Or I may choose to tap with no further instructions and no words.

Upsets are Like Little Movie Clips – Sometimes, I would explain that all our emotions show up as feelings in our body. Being upset can be like a very short video clip. I ask them to pretend that the upset feeling is a video clip they are watching in their body. This immediately distances them a bit from the incident. It is also a novel intervention, always more attention-getting to the children. I ask two non-invasive questions:

- ▶ **Where do you feel the upset in your body?** Whatever they say, I use their description as we tap the rounds.

- ▶ **How upset are you right this minute about it?** If the intensity is obviously very high, I assume a 10 and do not ask until they appear calmer. You could also use outstretched arms to measure the intensity.

- ▶ If the rapport was strong enough, I may ask: **If you wanted to give a name to the upsetting video what would it be?** This question assumes some level of cooperation and rapport with the child. I let them know they could use a simple code word, door, green, anger, ugly, etc.

- ▶ **Most of what upsets us can be in a really short clip. How long is your clip?** If longer than a minute or two, ask them to pick one scene to address.

- ▶ **How old are you in your video?** While I don't always ask this question, it does help clarify if they are upset about a present issue or if they are dealing with an earlier event that was triggered by the present.

Tapping with or Without Words – *"OK, just follow what I do."* I start tapping, and as I cover each point, if they had made comments, I repeat their words, e.g., *"this 9, anger, in my chest, I was 5, this TABLE video."* Using their words is another rapport builder; it proves you were listening, and he was heard. Sometimes to help focus—rarely a problem when they are upset—or if I had no information, I may say something like, *"Notice what you feel, this upset, see what you see, hear what you hear."*

Sometimes, they were willing to tap but didn't want to talk about it. That's OK. Tell them to focus on the area of the body where they feel upset. Since *tapping does the work*, and the words are to help keep focus, and an upset child, or for that matter adult, is *already* very focused! Don't be afraid to just tap; tapping with no words is effective.

Check the Progress – Tap for a few rounds until they appear calmer. Then, stop to remeasure the intensity. If I didn't get an intensity when we started, I say something like, *"If you were upset at a 10, on a scale of 0 to 10, when we started, what number would it be right now?"*

Sometimes the child would report he wasn't upset anymore. My goal was not "therapy" but to calm the child so that, hopefully, he would choose to return to the unit activities and interaction with staff and others. I would ask what he would like to do now. Usually, the choice was to go with the unit to an activity or to play with one of his buddies on the unit, show me one of his possessions, or ask me to play a game. If still upset, we'd continue until he was calm. He may or may not add something related: *It's so hard, it's not unfair, it makes me so mad, I hate him*, etc. In the next round(s), I would add whatever he had said.

No Pressure to Process – Never, ever, push anyone to continue to tap. Stop whenever they want. One of our goals for the residential program was to help the children be aware of what they felt and needed—to increase their sense of empowerment. Some want and seem to need, time to process things fully. Most, however, are glad to be calm and are ready to move on without much processing of what happened.

Practitioners and counselors learn to live with not knowing. It is part of respecting the client. Appreciate that you were able to assist someone in calming down and moving on from an upset. In doing so, you created one more experience that someone could care, and listen. You demonstrated a useful tool to calm, to have more control in life. That's a lot—all by itself.

About Respect – An important issue for working successfully with children or adults is respect.

- Respect indicates your belief that they have the ability to resolve their problems.

- Respect means you believe he or she is doing the best they can and will continue to do the best they can over time.

Yes, they may need support and assistance at times and may need new tools and resources—sometimes don't we all—but *our belief in their abilities and potential is powerful* stuff!

More about no words – Although we often use words to help us get specific and focused, once there, we might not need but one or two words, if any. Many practitioners and clients worry a great deal about what words to use. Gary Craig taught that words were only 10% of the effect of EFT. I believe it is an even less percentage. Roger Callahan, who developed Thought Field Therapy, stopped using words when tapping.

Nor does the client have to share intensity levels or details of what happened. This was a real challenge for some of the therapists at the residential program. They felt that the act of verbally *processing feelings* was an important, if not *the* critical part, of therapy. While I agree it can be helpful, never push, timing is everything. As I've repeated many times, we all have our own path, timing, and journey. Or as the name of Barry Stevens' book states: *Don't Push the River it Flows by Itself*.

After 40+ years of working with clients and supervising therapists, I am convinced that the quality of the relationship is a critical factor, perhaps *the* critical factor in successful outcomes. More important than processing is that the client feels heard and witnessed, respected, and valued, and that they have control in their life. The goal is to help them to modify perceptions and behaviors that are interfering with their lives. It is not always necessary to know what happened or what's behind it to accomplish that.

NOTES

Credit: Photo by Ashkan Forouzani from Unsplash

3

Introducing EFT to Your Clients

> **IN A NUTSHELL:** If you're reading this book, you have some experience using EFT, maybe even taken training. Still, you may struggle with how to integrate EFT into your existing practice. It seems so "odd" and "different," how will it go over with your clients? How much explaining do they need? How to start? The answer: Start simple. Focus on the body's response and tap.

It is possible to use only a small piece of the power of EFT to calm an anxious person without getting into the upsetting event(s) directly. Keep your explanation and your approach simple. After all, tapping is basically a relaxation technique. Here is a useful format. [Suggestions of wording are in italics.]

- ▶ Recognize They're Upset – *You seem really anxious today. Let's try a new exercise that has a high success rate for calming quickly.*

- ▶ Educate and Explain – *All emotions show up in our body. It is not possible to have an emotion without a corresponding body sensation. When we are the most upset, it's hard to have the energy and ability for effective problem-solving. If we calm the body, we calm the emotion, we can think more clearly.*

EFT IS SIMPLE—PEOPLE ARE COMPLEX

▶ **Preframe and Gain Permission** – *The goal is to calm the body by tapping lightly on acupuncture points—no needles. Are you game to try something a bit different? OK. We are going to focus on the body sensation you feel right now.*

▶ **Assess the Intensity** – *Close your eyes and take a breath. Check where in your body you feel the most upset.* You may need to give suggestions: *your stomach, your throat, your chest, etc. On a scale of 0 to 10 how intense is the feeling in that part of your body right now?* When they give their number—no matter what the number—just say, *that's fine. Now open your eyes and just follow what I do.*

▶ **Begin Tapping** – Tap the sequence of points and repeat the sequence at least three times using either one or both hands. Another option is to simply hold the point for a few seconds and take a breath at each point—this is a slower, even more, gentle process. Or depending on your profession and relationship with the client you could ask permission to tap *on* them.

> **Focus on the body and tap.**

▶ **Remind to Focus. Be reassuring.** – Tap with the client and use one simple reminder phrase at each point. *Just focus on what you feel in your body, all this anxiety, you're doing fine. That's right. Good job.* You do not need to know the issue for the tapping to be successful.

▶ **Reassess** – *OK, now close your eyes again and go back to the exact same part of the body you focused on before. What happened? Did the sensation move, did the intensity go up, stay the same, or go down? What number would you give it now? There is not a wrong answer. It is all just feedback.*

▶ **Reinforce and Celebrate** – Identify and reinforce changes. *That's great. In less than a minute you have cut your anxiety by __%.* Call their attention to any physical change you see. *You relaxed your shoulders and took a deep breath. Your leg is still. Your hands relaxed, etc.*

▶ Modify the Focus and Repeat – This exercise works most often to reduce the anxious feeling at least by half. Repeated rounds can bring even better results. Help them to *narrow the focus to one body sensation*; if they report more than one sensation, ask them to focus on the one that feels more prominent. **It is important to make sure the client is focusing on one specific detail of the body sensations.**

▶ It is unusual for EFT not to work at all. When you've made sure the focus is on *one* detail of the sensation and still no response, appreciate their willingness to try and discuss what the experience was like for them. Usually, another detail comes up that would be a useful focus for tapping and/or would make for a meaningful discussion.

▶ Whatever the outcome, ask for Feedback – *What did you experience as you were doing the tapping?* Ask about the issue they came in with that was creating the upset. Does it seem any different? At times, the tapping helped calm the response, but the client attributes the change to something else. It's not unusual to hear, "It wasn't that big a deal anyway."

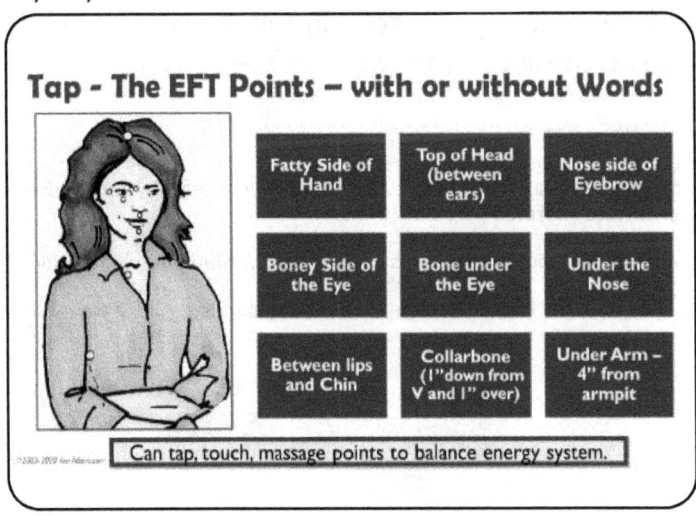

EFT IS SIMPLE—PEOPLE ARE COMPLEX

▶ Repeat tapping or stop to discuss the experience – Depending on the client's reaction to this exercise, you can continue tapping or continue the session in another therapeutic way.

▶ Educate and Encourage – *This is a new tool you can use for yourself. As soon as you notice any upset, you can tap. Tapping calms your body, which decreases the intensity of the emotion. You cannot be upset and calm at the same time, so focus on where in your body you feel upset as you tap. The calmer you are, the better you feel, and the better you see the options that are available to you.*

▶ At the end of the session – Give them a handout of the points. Discuss using EFT when they have an uncomfortable body response, i.e., any upset. *Catching your upset early will help prevent you from getting more upset. If you don't remember all the points, tap the ones you do remember. If you forget the order, tap in whatever order feels good to you. If one point seems to make the most difference, tap use that point more. What is important is focusing on the body sensation while you are doing the tapping.*

The process above uses one small part of EFT to calm anxiety. EFT is a powerful tool to add to any professional toolbox. EFT is powerful in reducing or negating the impact of trauma. Even a simple exercise like the above is useful—all by itself.

NOTES

Reminder: If you are a licensed professional, check your organization's guidelines as to what constitutes informed consent.

To Download a handout of EFT Points go to - https://AnnAdams.com/Handout-points

Credit: Slide from the EFT4PowerPoint EFT training package - EFT4PowerPoint.com

4

How Does EFT Work?

> IN A NUTSHELL: We can see *what* EFT does, but we still don't understand exactly how. David Feinstein, Ph.D., gave a talk at an ACEP Conference in Santa Clara, CA, discussing the ongoing research as to the effectiveness of EFT. As to the *"how"* EFT works, Dr. Feinstein gave my favorite answer to date.

Brain scans from fMRIs and other measures show changes in the body chemistry and brain activity after using EFT. We can see some of *what EFT does: it impacts the body in various ways to calm the physical reactions*. However, we still don't know *how* EFT creates those changes. Feinstein said that there is agreement among practitioners on the *effectiveness of pairing two things: focusing on the issue and utilizing an energy intervention*. And, in my observation, some don't agree with even those.

All the rest of what is effective in utilizing any meridian technique is not clear. *What* exactly is *it* that works? *How* does *it* create the change? What we do know is, as David Feinstein put it so beautifully, "Something unknown is doing who knows what." We don't know. Some of the current explanations as to what causes the changes:

- Magical, special, different – out "there"
- A Placebo – thinking it will work
- Distraction – takes the mind off your issue or pain
- Calms during exposure – EFT relaxes the body
- Cognitive Restructuring – create new perceptions
- Addresses the "Thought Field"
- Intention – from both client and practitioner
- Spiritual healing – like prayer—a co-creation

> "Something unknown is doing who knows what."
> - David Feinstein

Most of the above ideas, however, cover the *what*, not the *how*. We do not yet know for sure. Fortunately, we do not *have* to understand how it works to use it effectively. After all, it took from the early 1800s until the late 1960s for scientists to understand how aspirin worked.* We used aspirin anyway. We can see the effect and benefit of the impact of EFT without knowing why or how.

Until we have more information, "Something unknown is doing who knows what!" will have to do. We still have a lot to learn about the body, and we *are* working on learning it. Maybe someday we will be crystal clear. Just not yet.

NOTES

*Even when we do know how it may still not be clear to everyone. For example, in the article on History of Aspirin, Wikipedia states, "Later research [after 1971] showed that NSAIDs such as aspirin works by inhibiting cyclooxygenase, the enzyme responsible for converting arachidonic acid into a prostaglandin." Got that??

5

Your Space Reflects Your Values

> **IN A NUTSHELL:** Take a fresh look at your environment from the client perspective; it may surprise you. Whether you call where you work an office, consulting room, or therapy room, it is an important part of the client's experience with you. It is a reflection of your values, your respect for the client, and yourself.

I remember a therapist's office that, as I passed, I shuddered. It was cluttered and sloppy looking. Furniture looked like a reject from a thrift shop. Papers were everywhere, on the floor, the window ledge and stacked on the table she used as a desk, along with used tissues, candy wrappers, food containers, and three coffee cups that looked as if they had been there for weeks. Yuck! And trust me, I am not a neat freak! As I left the building, I saw that therapist, who looked as unkempt as her office. Maybe she was an excellent therapist, but she'd have "lost" me as a client at the door of her office. This is unfortunate and much more common than one would expect.

An article in *Psychology Today* written about what made a welcoming environment, written by a client who did not make another appointment, felt that *if the therapist didn't value her surroundings, on some level that translated to her not valuing the client either.*

In a research study using pictures of various therapist offices the characteristic getting the highest ratings were neat and orderly, decorated with soft touches like pillows and throw rugs, and featuring a few personal touches like diplomas and framed photos. Our workspace, like preparing our house for sale, should be uncluttered, neat, in good repair, and not overly personal. Healthy plants can help, too, if the combined number of them is not equivalent to a jungle!

What do your clients see?

Some therapists, like the obviously successful owner of this office, put pictures of their office on their web site. Granted your space doesn't have to look this lovely or expensive, but notice how pleasant, neutral, and comfortable it is. You don't need any other convincing to think that whoever is in that office is a successful professional who values his surroundings—and his clients. Neat, orderly, throw pillows and rug, and a few personal touches on the table. I bet the diplomas are on the wall as well.

What your space looks like matters even if you see clients using video software. Are you aware of the background your online client may see? Is your bed or breakfast dishes or other clutter in the background? Keep it neat. Better yet, have a screen that separates your workspace from your living space. Think your space doesn't matter if you only use the phone? Think again. What *you* are looking at impacts you; it still matters.

It is normal after a while to stop *really* seeing our space. Try this. Go to where your client would come in. Notice what your client may see as they approach. Then, sit where the client sits. Is it comfortable? Is what you see neat and orderly? Ask a friend—one of your "tell it like it is" friends—to pretend they are the client and share how they experience your office environment.

Anything Jarring to the Senses?

How about the entrance? Is the doorway cleaned and swept? Is the carpet or other flooring in good repair? Is there enough light? Are the kid's toys or other clutter all over the yard or entrance? On my way to a hairdresser's space in her home, I had to wind my way through all the storage and clutter in her garage. [No, I didn't go back.] What other parts of the building would they see on the way to, and in, your office? What do they smell? Fish or cabbage you just cooked? I did Rolfing in one practitioner's home with a strong mildew smell. When I mentioned it to the practitioner, she dismissed it, saying she didn't notice.

Is there a need for signage? I had to hunt one practitioner who was in an office with a lot of other therapists. No list of occupants was posted.

Is your space quiet and devoid of interruptions? Family instructed not to interrupt while in session? Kids bribed to be quiet? Made sure any deliveries aren't supposed to come during a session time? Put the phone on auto answer? Better yet—turn it off. Put the dog/cat up? If you believe the pet to be useful for your clients do you check that supposition with each client?

Speaking of phones, what number do you give your clients? If it's your mobile phone are you in a confidential environment when you answer it? Who else answers your phone? Have you trained them on how to respond; what to say? I called for an appointment with a Yoga teacher. Her teenage son, rather angry sounding, answered with a curt, "I'm on the other line, what do you want?" Another time the practitioner answered politely, but the children were in some a loud, unhappy discussion.

And, oh yes, if you see clients in your home office and need to share your bathroom, put the personal items up and remove your favorite ratty robe out from behind the door. I saw that in a massage therapist's home office. Shows you are human, yes, but does nothing for seeing you as a knowledgeable professional whose key focus is the client.

Attractive environments don't make you an excellent practitioner nor guarantee a client's return, but the space, however humble, matters. It should be inviting, clean, neat, and comfortable.

6

Upside and Downside of Being Real

IN A NUTSHELL: How much of yourself should you disclose? Is self-disclosure necessary to create the rapport and relationship for the client to feel safe to go deeply into the issues? Yes and no. As is often the case, the answer depends on the client. But, what are the guidelines?

Charlie asks, "What do you like to do?" I smile and answer, "One of the things I like to do is to call a friend and meet at the park to take a walk or go watch a game." A couple of months later, Gene asks the same question, "What do you like to do when you are not working?" I turned it back to him, "Let's explore the challenges *you* have with your days off."

> **You can be too real.**

My initial training for clinical social work in the '70s gave the message that any sharing of personal information should be "kept to a minimum and carefully selected." In the last 20 years, this instruction has been modified. The consensus now is that *appropriate and well-timed self-disclosure is helpful to the client.*

Whether appropriate and well-timed or minimum and carefully selected, what are the guidelines?

Is there a line?
Where is the line?
What kind of line?

Two key factors for consideration:

Intention – *why* are you sharing this information about yourself.

Authenticity – what you do and say and think are coherent.

The challenge with authenticity is you can be authentic and still overshare: you can be *too real.*

- You can be *too real* and not be effective with a client who then suffers from *too much irrelevant information that may slow progress.*

- You can be *too real,* and the client can *sidestep his or her issues.*

- You can be *too real* and *create a role reversal;* the client feels the need to take care of you. Many abused people have been, literally, trained to take care of others and can do so in very subtle ways you may miss; *they will put their real needs aside.*

- You can be *too real,* and the client feels the need to *"protect you" from their pain,* and simply goes only as deep as they believe *you* can handle.

Experience helps, of course, but these challenges are some of the many, many reasons practitioners are encouraged to continue to do their own work. Only exploring and becoming aware of your blocks, and attempt to resolve and mitigate them, will help you to sidestep potential minefields, set boundaries, and know when being real is genuinely authentic.

Increasing your awareness of the impact of your own issues increases your ability, to be honest with yourself about your intention for self-disclosure.

To Share, Not to Share?

When you are tempted to share a personal feeling, thought, or story ask yourself:

What is my purpose? How is that purpose related to moving this client toward their goals?

▶ When you are tempted to ask out of simple curiosity, check yourself, "Will this question move this client toward more clarity and their goals, or am I simply curious?"

▶ Most clients are naturally curious about us as people. When a client asks a question about you or your thoughts, ask yourself:

- **Will my answer be useful for this client?**

- **Is this an "honest" question that will help the client move toward his goals?**

- **Is it a legitimate question that the client has a right to know, e.g. your experience?**

- **Is it a diversionary tactic to avoid a feeling or looking at their issues?**

- **Is it an attempt to move your *role* to one of friend versus practitioner?**

Charlie, who came in with relationship challenges, was extremely shy, with few social skills, had difficulty organizing his world to include others. He was struggling with what to do. He was terrified that he would get into a situation that would go beyond his communication skills.

His question as to what I liked to do was an honest concern; he wanted some suggestions and examples as to how to navigate the social world. He was at a loss of how to be with people in a non-threatening way for himself. He needed education in addition to tapping. His response to my going to the park was that inviting someone to meet him somewhere public was scary. "What are you feeling in your body as you think about that?" I asked. As we tapped for his body sensations his fear calmed. We were able to address an event he remembered attending when he was ridiculed. We spent the rest of the session talking about options he was considering and ways to deal with social challenges.

If I thought/felt Charlie was avoiding something, I would have shifted the question back to him as I did with Gene. Gene also had many relationship challenges. He was very needy, self-absorbed, and dependent; he wore people out. Gene frequently tried to shift our relationship to that of a dependent friendship. When he asked, "What do you like to do on your days off?" it could have been interpreted to mean that he was beginning to show interest in what others did. At that point, I seriously doubted it.

My response turned the question back to him to help explore how he could do fun things on his days off without being so demanding of others; how he could learn to enjoy his own company. He found an important memory when he'd tried to be on his own and failed. Tapping through that event brought him one step closer to his goal of feeling a confident worthwhile person.

Helpful Guidelines

- If it is an honest question delivered in an honest moment, answer it. Answer it with the minimum amount of detail and the maximum amount of tact the moment calls for. *Questions about you by the client are still very much about*

UPSIDE AND DOWNSIDE OF BEING REAL

the client's issues. Do not embellish.

- If it is a diversionary tactic or some level of inappropriate curiosity about you, politely turn it back to them. *Why do you ask?*

- *If it is simply your curiosity, sit on it.* Make sure the questions you ask are designed to move the client forward. Would the question help guide the client to the next step?

- If it is a temptation to share a story or your own reaction, ask yourself *what is the real reason you want to share?* Early in my training, we were taught to be more of a "blank slate" to the client; in today's therapy world, the expectation is that you are more "real" and friendly. However, it remains true that the session is about the client's issues, not yours!

There are definite benefits to self-disclosure. On the positive side, sharing an example of your experience may help give clients options and encouragement to try new things. It may deepen rapport. It may normalize his experience. Just make sure your *intention is to help move the client toward their personal goals.*

NOTES

Credits:
Share or Not to Share Photo by Tumisu on Pixabay
Line Photo by Daniel Olah on Pixabay

7

What is the Purpose of Sneaking Up?

> IN A NUTSHELL: "If Tearless Trauma Technique (TTT) and Chasing the Pain techniques are effective in keeping the intensity low," one practitioner asked, "What is the purpose of Sneaking Up?" A good question. I commend her for studying the EFT process in enough depth to ask that question. The answer: Sneaking Up is more a concept than a technique and does not have a clear definition or process. Indeed, Gary Craig, in his online tutorial, merely mentions the concept.

All EFT techniques have a key goal in common—to address issues and emotions as painlessly as possible. All EFT techniques intend to minimize emotional pain by slowly going deeper; in essence, to always "sneak up" on our problem.

EFT is used to move the client gradually, and comfortably, toward increasingly intense aspects by initially addressing less intense details. Gary designed all the EFT techniques to minimize the amount of distress for the client. EFT International* follows this concept; its Glossary states, "*Sneaking Up is a strategy of carefully approaching a problem to minimize the level of pain and suffering for the client.*"

Any tactic that does not address the issue directly but goes slowly closer to a painful event is "sneaking up." Sneaking Up is

- tiptoeing up to the issue
- circling it
- taking the edge off
- gradually spiraling in closer
- putting some distance between client and issue
- addressing a separate but related less intense aspect
- addressing the feelings around addressing the issue
- tapping for body sensations

Gary called Tearless Trauma, Chasing the Pain, and Sneaking Up the "Gentle Techniques" since these methods, like the constricted breathing exercise and addressing specific body sensations, do not seem to address the issue directly. They are options for "protective distancing" to help protect clients from high intensity and to slow down until they feel comfortable to address the issue more directly. These techniques also have an opportunity to bypass cognitive resistance.

EFT International also categorizes addressing the body sensations and using image metaphors as gentle techniques. The goal is to lower the intensity around the issue before addressing an issue more directly as with the Movie Technique and Tell the Story.** The Movie and Story can be utilized as gentle techniques by additionally addressing only the title of the "movie," then going slowly and methodically toward the more highly emotional points.

WHAT IS THE PURPOSE OF SNEAKING UP?

How did Sneaking Up gain status as one of the EFT techniques?

In searching www.emofree.com for Sneaking Up, it is mentioned in only a couple of sentences in both the original and the current tutorial on his web site. Three techniques are listed as *"Ways to inject more gentleness into the procedure:"* The Tearless Trauma Technique, Chasing the Pain, and Sneaking Up on the problem.

For a week in August 2004, Gary invited 14 EFT trainers, including myself, from several countries to his home in Northern California overlooking the coastline to explore the possibility of establishing training guidelines for EFT. We sat around his sunken living room, creating a list of the key concepts in EFT. In retrospect, I wish we had also spent time *clearly defining* each technique and concept and explaining its purpose. It would have saved a lot of questions.

That meeting spawned the EFT Training Guidelines. While Gary no longer publishes the guidelines, they still make up much of the structure of the EFT International Standards and other EFT accreditation or certification training programs. Also spawned from that meeting was my first revision of the EFT4PowerPoint Training Package, created for planning and conducting an EFT training class to be faster and easier.

Suggestions for Sneaking Up
Strong Emotions Not Necessary

1. General approach:
   "The Big One"
2. Rank Intensity of Physical Response
3. Tap for a General:
   "Even though I have this discomfort..."
4. Take the edge off
5. Gradually spiral in closer
6. General tapping, more specific - repeat

© 2004 Ann Adams

EFT IS SIMPLE—PEOPLE ARE COMPLEX

Since my EFT4PowerPoint program was already reflective of the decisions made by the Sea Ranch group, Gary asked if I would modify my existing program slightly to fit those guidelines. In exchange, he said he would recommend it on the emofree.com site. For the next few weeks, we debated every-single-word! The above slide, from the 2004 EFT4PowerPoint version, reflects Gary's original wording developed from our many discussions about the wording for each concept.

> NOTE: Gary Craig is no longer involved with any workshop guidelines or recommendations. However, when the guidelines and program were completed, he did give the EFT4PowerPoint a testimonial on his site: *"This PowerPoint presentation is an easy step-by-step way to conduct EFT Workshops. It would cost over $3,000 of your time to recreate this quality presentation. HIGHLY RECOMMENDED!!"* – Gary Craig, 2005

EFT4PowerPoint V3020 is the fifth update. It reflects the increased emphasis in the EFT world for client safety and increased focus on body sensations. It reflects all the EFT International Guidelines—and still includes the original presentation with Gary's original wording!

NOTES

Credit: *EFT International, an accrediting body for EFT Practitioners. https://eftinternational.com

**See EFT Level 1 and 2 Review for definitions of these concepts.

Slides by the author.

For more information about the training package, see www.EFT4PowerPoint.com

Drawing of girl by Kari Reed for the EFT4PowerPoint.com package.

8

Missed Opportunities

> **IN A NUTSHELL:** Occasionally, a client will confront us or give us uncomfortable feedback. How we respond can impact a client in many ways, pro and con, and can make all the difference in whether the client returns.

Years ago, before EFT, my neighbor, "Jane," a single mom divorced for a year, took her 7-year-old son to a children's mental health clinic in a nearby university. The clinic required the family to participate; Jane dutifully rearranged her and the children's schedule. For three sessions, they took a bunch of tests and did exercises that Jane did not see as relevant. Nor did she believe the clinic or the young female psychologist was addressing her son's problem in school. She felt the family were guinea pigs for reasons she didn't understand. As she attempted to explain her frustrations to the young psychologist who was in her last placement in a teaching facility before finalizing her Ph.D., about the experience to date, Jane ended saying, "You look like my babysitter."

The young psychologist took these remarks very personally. She acted miffed, gave a defensive response along the lines of "seems we can't work together," and terminated the session without attempting to address Jane's issues, give a referral, or make suggestions for the future. *This is an example of not creating a safe, comfortable connection in which to work!*

The helping field recognizes the reality of transference and countertransference, which in an oversimplified nutshell, means that the client projects his past experiences on you, and you project your past experiences on him.

In this case, the psychologist was triggered by her insecurity. Clearly, this psychologist had not yet done "her own work" sufficiently to be able to set her feelings aside. Clearly, the psychologist had not explained what to expect and what the tests were for and what would happen afterward.

What a golden opportunity this young psychologist missed to address Jane's overall lack of feeling of support, a feeling there was no one to ask for help, always having to meet everyone else's expectations, always being the caregiver, with an already overloaded schedule. Jane was an overwhelmed single mom with no frame of reference for what was happening. She didn't see that rearranging her family's schedule and adding in the long trip to the clinic every week to their already too busy life was helpful to her son and the other children.

WHAT IF…?

Jane wasn't interested in being a guinea pig for someone's certification, which is how it appeared to her. She wanted help with options for her son's problems in school. After several visits, Jane felt misunderstood and used. What if the clinic and the psychologist had ensured that Jane understood the clinic process and that she understood how the testing would be useful? What if Jane's goals were clarified and addressed throughout the sessions? What if the psychologist had worked through enough of her insecurity issues and was *not* defensive? What if she'd addressed Jane's comment differently?

▶ With respect and genuine curiosity:

"Oh! So, you go through a process that doesn't seem meaningful to you and haven't gotten help solving the problems that brought you here. What do you see you most need right now?"

▶ Or emphatic:

"That has to be tough for you. You came for help but are not seeing how you can get it from what we've been doing and from someone so young who reminds you of your babysitter. Do I have that right?"

▶ Or, honest feedback:

"Sounds sort of like you don't know me well enough yet to trust me to be different than your babysitter—does that fit? What would you need to know about me or the process to feel more comfortable?"

▶ Or, asking the client to take personal responsibility:

"That's got to be tough to feel that way. How do you think we should work through this?"

Any of the above statements would have continued to work on connection and would have recognized and respected Jane's view. Such comments would have been unexpected by Jane, broken the "like my babysitter" view, and had a good chance of shifting Jane's perspective. She did want help for her son. She did not see how the clinic would help.

...and, the rest of the story

Jane was angry and determined to find other resources and options to help her son. She went back to her son's teacher, asking for other recommendations to help him catch up. Jane found a scholarship with a tutoring agency. She asked some moms she respected but didn't yet know well to share how they would handle the issue.

She checked her local library. One of the books recommended was Thomas Gordon's *Parent Effectiveness Training*. [The 2000 edited edition remains an excellent book.] She was excited about the problem-solving sections and implemented some of the ideas.

EFT IS SIMPLE—PEOPLE ARE COMPLEX

She began having weekly family meetings and set guidelines. She allowed the children to call an emergency family meeting when they felt the need. Her son grew up to be a responsible citizen and graduated magna cum laude from college. And Jane? She gained friends and confidence and went back to school herself.

People may be more resilient and resourceful than we sometimes think they are!

NOTES

A link to purchase Thomas Gordon's *Parent Effectiveness Training* is listed on www.annadams.com/resources along with other valuable resources both free and for purchase.

9

Does One Size Ever Fit All?

> **IN A NUTSHELL:** There are many good suggestions for establishing rapport with clients—but at times, contradictory suggestions. The complexity and individuality of people at times can make developing rapport challenging. The only truly universal practice is to deeply listen to their verbal and non-verbal communication. What works for this client, with this problem, at this time? Listen deeply, and adapt to create an individualized approach that fits each client's mindset, experiences, and culture.

You study, watch videos, seek guidance from experienced practitioners; you begin to see differences of opinion, approach, perception, and methods among the experts. *What is the right thing to do?*

Advice for establishing rapport and a safe environment for a client frequently contains suggestions such as *maintaining eye contact,* asking our clients to *take a deep breath, using their words, playing soothing music* in the background, or asking the client to *draw a picture* of their issue. We've certainly been told to *exude warmth and empathy*! As EFTers, we are taught to *find a specific event and tap through the details.* All these approaches *can be the right thing*—at the right time, with the right client—to help the client to feel safe, to go deeper. *But—not always!*

Some commonly shared suggestions, with some clients, **could be detrimental.**

- Eye contact "can be" perceived as threatening to some clients. Consistent eye contact is not acceptable in every culture.

- Using their words to reflect what they just said "can be" seen as mockery.

- Asking someone to breathe deeply, who has experienced a trauma in which taking a deep breath would have been dangerous, *"can be"* triggering. Asking the client to take a *comfortable breath* can be more acceptable.

> **One size never fits all.**

- Playing music "can be" interpreted as abandoning the client or be a trigger.

- Drawing "can be" an immediate throwback to a time in which they felt a total failure and intense disapproval.

- Humming a particular tune "can be" triggering.

- The act of tapping itself "can be" triggering. One practitioner working with tsunami victims reported they weren't willing to tap, telling her that EFT triggers "the waves coming at me."

- Unexpected warmth and empathy "can be" frightening to a client with a fear of intimacy.

- Tapping "can be" interpreted as distracting. Or a slower, more introspective Touch and Breathe approach would be preferred. Or they may want someone to simply listen to them or maybe just vent some of their feelings and frustrations first.

- Pushing for a specific "can be" off-putting when they do

not want to or are unable to get to a specific event, at least for now.

- Some clients expect questions, others may see questions as invasive.
- Some need time to share their feelings and story and become more comfortable with you and the process before addressing *any* issue.
- Some do not want to tap—period.
- Others have been tapping seemly forever, and they—and perhaps their body as well—want to do something else.

What's a practitioner to do?

With all the variations in people and approaches, there is a guideline for every session, for every client—adaptation. Develop the ability to be comfortable with different relationships, different approaches, all the while remaining who you are.

Pay close attention to everything they do or say and *how* they do or do not say and do it. Calibrate body language, tone of voice, periods of silence or being hyper-verbal, etc. This hour's client may have an entirely different need or expectation or want a different approach to their problem than your previous client who was dealing with a similar problem.

"...clients, not [practitioners], make [your approach] work. [Sessions] should be organized around [their] resources, perceptions, experiences, and ideas ... following their lead; adopting their language, world view, goals and ideas about the problem; and acknowledge their experiences with, and inclinations about, the change process."*

EFT IS SIMPLE—PEOPLE ARE COMPLEX

> **One size never fits all.**

The *most effective practitioners take the time to gather sufficient information about the client to be able to vary their approach. Or, to recognize when a client would be better served by a different approach or modality or another helping person* with a different approach or level of expertise. No matter how much we care or how many skills we have, the painful truth is that we cannot help *all* the people *all* the time. Sometimes, this client is not a match for how you work, and it's best to refer.

> **No one can be all things to all people.**

Resource: *The Skilled Helper, 11th Edition* by Gerard Egan. Available on Amazon.com. A valuable how-to book for working successfully with the multitude of complexities that people may bring for all levels of practitioner. Many useful suggestions and examples that you can put to use, whatever your approach. If you haven't got it, get it. Read it. If you have read it, read it again. It's that helpful.

NOTES

Credits: *Egan, Gerard, (2010). *The Skilled Helper*, ninth edition.

10

EFT Shortcut – Ace-in-the-Hole

> **IN A NUTSHELL:** All tapping modalities have specific instructions: for best results, do this, then this, then that, etc. Modifying those instructions and creating shortcuts is common and began with the very first "tapper" in the 1970s, Roger Callahan, developer of Thought Field Therapy. He created shortcuts for TFT, algorithms for specific emotions. Since that time many tapping variations have been shown to be effective.

Callahan believed it was important to "diagnose" which meridian point to tap and in what order, using a series of muscle tests on alarm points. This "prescription" for the tapping sequence could be lengthy. In developing his system for relieving or negating upsetting emotions, he began seeing common patterns for which points and in what order, leading him to develop algorithms. The algorithms were a list of points most often identified for specific emotions, e.g., anxiety, depression, grief. One of the TFT algorithms identified for anxiety was just three points: collarbone (C), eye (E), underarm (A) followed by the 9 Gamut, and repeated.

When first introduced to energy psychology, I was searching for other effective tools for helping the children in the residential treatment facility. I wanted something simple that our always anxious children could remember. By rearranging the TFT anxiety algorithm from C-E-A to A-C-E and skipping the 9 Gamut, I tested the rearranged algorithm on myself and my friends. When convinced it was effective, I taught these three points to the children as their "Ace-in-a-Hole." Even if the concept of Ace-in-a-Hole was not a familiar metaphor, they all learned the simple process quickly. It worked well to quickly decrease their level of anxiety. These points can be addressed not only by directly tapping on them but in a stealthy way allowing the children to use it anywhere unobserved.

A - Scratch under their arm.

C - Hold their hand to the chest and take a breath.

E - Rub the bone under the eye.

"Callie" was an angry, often aggressive teenager. Given her history, she had reason to be. When confronted with her behavior after an altercation with another child, she said, as many of the acting out children claim, "She/he made me so angry, *I couldn't help it.*" Maybe, maybe not. I'd reply with some version of, "Must be tough to feel that out of control. How much less trouble would you get into if you got angry *only when you really wanted to be* angry?" We would talk about noticing what happens in her body *before* losing control and practiced stealthy A-C-E.

One of my challenges with TFT was the focus on identifying an emotion. The children often experienced several conflicting emotions at the same time and/or were not able to clearly label their feelings. We are not born knowing that a particular body sensation means you have "X" emotion. We are taught what to call a body reaction.

Emotions are energy. Many labeled emotions have similar body sensations. Is it even possible to give a *specific* name to each? For instance, the body sensations for excitement and anxiety are similar. *Maybe we should look at our label of the emotion as a metaphor for the body sensation.* Maybe everything we tap for is a representation, a metaphor for something else. For instance, we are not tapping for an event—it is over—we are tapping for the memory of the event, the impact of the event. We know we have an emotion because our body reacts, maybe by "shutting down" allowing no feeling at all. *Maybe all roads lead to the body.*

Early in my practice of tapping, I came to the same conclusion Gary Craig did—the order of points doesn't matter, *maybe not even which points you use*. Clients can often identify "one point" that seems more effective for them than other points.

Besides, we've dropped points in the development of EFT. In TFT, the ring finger point was skipped because the Gamut spot covered it. Gary stopped using the liver point because it was more difficult to reach for women. When he dropped the gamut exercise, he didn't add in the ring finger. Sometimes simply tapping one point is all that is needed. So obviously skipping some points could be effective. Or maybe simply imagining tapping them. I've led groups in just imagining tapping the points with effective results. After coming out of retirement, in 2010, Gary introduced "The Unseen Therapist," a system that does not require tapping at all.

John Diamond, a psychiatrist from Australia now living in New York, worked closely with George Goodheart, the chiropractor who is credited with identifying the connections between meridians, muscle reaction, and emotions. His work influenced Callahan. Diamond offers an outline as to which meridian addressed what emotion. Diamond's theory is interesting, at times useful, but with Diamond's theory we are back to having to identify which emotion—not always an easy task for many, *and* not everyone's body seems to respond in the same way.

The ultimate shortcut is using just one point. Acupuncturists believe that since the meridians are all connected it is possible that only one needle is effective. I asked my local acupuncturist about this. She said she had seen it done; she did not, as yet, have the nerve to try it. Finding one point that is often more responsive as you tap, would be the shortest tapping sequence! What's yours? My personal favorite is the underarm point. Gary told one audience his favorite was the collarbone.

It is important to know the "rules" of EFT, of any technique, before modifying them. The Art of Delivery is knowing when to do what with each issue, and when to follow the rules, when to modify them, and when to toss it all out the window and do something else. I'm convinced that there are many "roads" to resolving our issues.

NOTES

Credit: Ace photo by Daniel Rykhev on Unsplash.com
All roads… from EFT4PowerPoint Training Package, EFT4PowerPoint.com

11

Assessing Intensity and Clarity

> **IN A NUTSHELL:** The intensity of the emotion is a key indicator of what approach you will use and how slow or fast you go. The intensity the client reports, however, is not the only factor to keep in mind as you work with someone; clarity of the issue is also a factor.

The EFT Flow Chart was created for a weekend EFT Class. Earlier in the day, a student asked, *"Is there a flow chart for when to use which EFT technique."* Hmmm?? Always on the lookout for more interesting and simple ways to teach EFT, I gave it some thought. Well, why isn't there? That night I fell asleep thinking about his question. I woke about 3 am with the concept formed and immediately drew a rough draft.

The students loved it. My newsletter readers loved it. Of the multitude of handouts I've shared with others over the years, this is hands down the most popular. People do love "systems" that offer a 1-2-3 solution to a problem—remember this when you are marketing your products and services!

The Flow Chart has been a useful guideline, especially for EFT beginning practitioners. It's been downloaded from my web site hundreds, maybe thousands, of times. But no flow chart, no strategy, is ever 100% for every client every time.

EFT IS SIMPLE—PEOPLE ARE COMPLEX

EFT can be simple; people are complex.* Using any technique depends on the client and their situation and timing. Know your client!

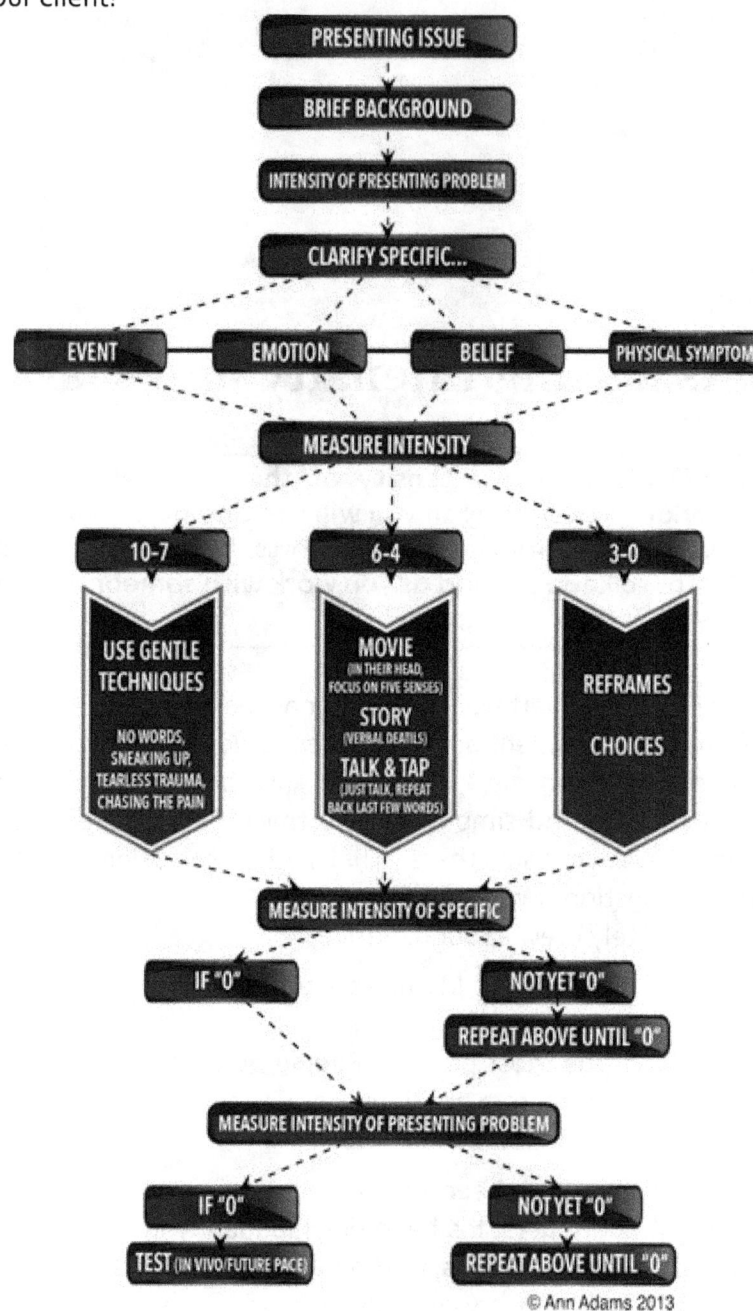

ASSESSING INTENSITY AND CLARITY

During an interview with Judy Wolvington, who conducted interviews on EFTRadioOnline for several years, she commented that the EFT Flow Chart was, "One of the best tools for EFT that I've seen."** Download a copy at https://www.AnnAdams.com/FlowChart.

Consider Intensity *and* Clarity – The client's level of awareness, of clarity concerning the presenting problem, is another important factor to consider in deciding which technique to use when. The less clarity the client has concerning their issue, the more complex working with the client may be. The more rapport, *timely* detective work, and the slower you need to go.

EFT Master, Gwyneth Moss created a useful table for assessing and considering how clear, how aware someone is of their issue, and offers suggestions for addressing each layer.

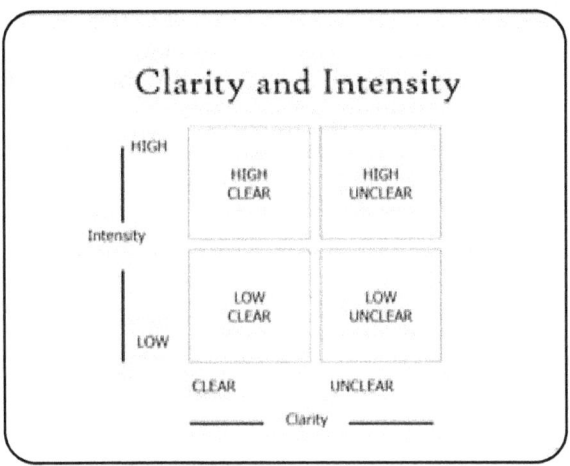

- Low Intensity

    o Clarity High – They know the problem and the roots. Go for the problem. Tap for triggers and memories.

    o Clarity Low – Use communication skills and gentle techniques to elicit information and connect. Low intensity *and* low clarity can be the most challenging situation for practitioners—in any field—and needs a lot of patience.

- High Intensity
    - Clarity High – They may know what happened but could become overwhelmed. May need continuous tapping and reassurance. Contain intensity with gentle techniques, sneak up, use body feelings. Don't address the issue directly until they feel ready. Issues can be complex with many aspects and layers. Again, patience. When the client is ready, thoroughly address the tiny sensory details, work around the edges of the problem with trivial aspects or concerns. When memories do appear, address them *very gently*. Refer when necessary.
    - Clarity Low – Go slowly, lots of patience. Use positive language to help them envisage the possibility of change. Work with little things and little changes. Let the bigger things emerge in their own time for clearing, *don't rush*. There will be some big false truths, shocks, and periods of stress to clear. Ask about similar times in their life. Tap around the problem using their exact words. Look for those "false truths," then address when and where these beliefs may have originated.

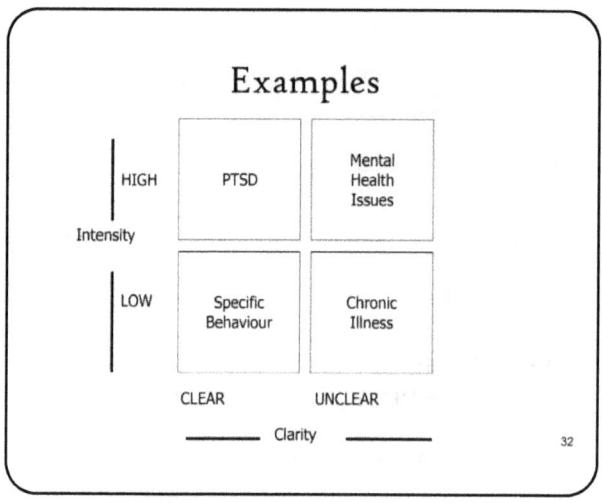

ASSESSING INTENSITY AND CLARITY

NOTES

Credit:
*An Annism – EFT can be simple; people can be complex.

**Download a copy at https://www.AnnAdams.com/FlowChart

Thanks to Gwyneth Moss, EFT Founding Master, for the concept and the slides. EFT-Helps.com

The interview with Judy Wolvington is on her website: unleashyourauthenticpower.com TAB Events, TAB EFT Radio, page 10. There are many other useful interviews on the website.

12

When Amy Gets Upset

> **IN A NUTSHELL:** When sharing information with our clients about how the brain works and what happens in our body when we get upset, our client's eyes may glaze over. They become lost in the unfamiliar words: Amygdala, Hypothalamus, Pituitary Gland, Frontal Cortex, Adrenalin, Epinephrine, etc. Here is a, granted oversimplified, story that may be more understandable.

Our body is like a community, and several members play a critical role in creating our upsetting reactions: four in the brain, one just outside the brain, and one on top of the kidneys. All of these parts work together. Let's give them nicknames.

Once a threat, real or imagined, is identified by Frank, the prefrontal cortex, or Liz, our brain stem, they send a message to Amy, the amygdala. Amy is small and has only one very important job, to broadcast the alarm whenever a message of "danger" is received. Amy responds whether the "threat" is a real external threat to the body or "self," or merely *perceived internally* as threatening.

Amy receives a message and sends a warning—sort of like turning all the lights on in the house in the middle of the night. Then, like a local volunteer fire department, Thal, the hypothalamus, is nearby and sees those blazing lights and immediately informs Pete, the pituitary gland. Pete begins making and distributing emergency chemicals, getting the body ready for fight or flight. One of those chemicals wakes up Andy, a more distant neighbor, the adrenal gland, who then begins to release the storehouse of "ammunition" necessary for the other parts of the body to maximize their ability to fight or flee.

Let's look at that process again: Amy is triggered to turn on the alarm by the message from Liz or Frank. It could be just the perception of outside danger by Liz, the earliest resident of the brain, who's very old and not always a team player. An example of *outside* danger would be walking along the street. You hear a dog bark very close by. It sounds big and vicious. Instantaneously, you are alert, your heart pounds, your breath becomes shallow, you sweat—all from Amy's (your amygdala) signal. Your body reacts when Thal signals Pete and Andy (i.e., the hypothalamus sends chemical messages to the pituitary and adrenal glands.) Liz (your brain stem) reacts immediately. When you realize the large dog is behind a tall fence, only then does Frank (your prefrontal cognitive part of the brain) give the message… "you are safe," and the body calms.

Or perhaps it is an "inside" danger; Frank had a negative thought, or something happened that, while currently not a threat, seems to Frank to be a similar situation in which there *was* actual danger either to the physical body *or to the sense of identity*. Any negative, limiting thought, "Let's not try that again, it hurt too much last time," or "Oh, no!" or "You can't do that," or "Doing that is too risky," etc. are also messages to Amy to hit that alarm.

Amy is a key part of an instinctive powerful, primitive, and automatic defense system, the first within the body to respond to any threat—real or perceived. Amy does *not* question, assess, or evaluate the meaning of the threatening "message"—again, real or perceived. Amy *responds*.

The amygdala (Amy) simply turns on the alarm. It is then the hypothalamus (Thal) alerts the pituitary gland (Pete), who then sends a chemical warning to the adrenal glands (Andy) to start pumping chemicals throughout the body. With the increase of these chemicals, the body tends to become anxious and fearful—maybe even panicked.

Whose job is it to evaluate the situation, to decide if there is a *real* danger or if it is a false message? Not Liz or Amy or Thal, or Pete or Andy!

The prefrontal cortex (Frank) is responsible for problem solving and judgment. Frank can be very rational, logical, and reality-oriented. Frank *could* evaluate whether the danger is real or false—as happens all too often with folks who have chronic panic attacks or anxiety. The problem? When the body is on high alert, highly emotional, Frank cannot function well. He assesses the situation *after* the danger is gone. As long as there is, real or perceived, inside or outside, danger, the resources of the body are diverted. Frank is "put on hold." Frank loses much of his cognitive abilities. All this means we are not thinking clearly when aroused or upset.

Chemicals like epinephrine flowing within the body convince Frank that there really *is* danger; *it sure feels like it!* Frank shuts down to leave as much energy as possible for the rest of the body to react. Now the body is on a chemically propelled loop of a roller coaster ride—the voluntary fire department is spraying chemicals everywhere.

At what point does Frank look at the reality of the situation and tell Amy to back down, "Nope, just kidding, false alarm?" That is part of the problem. We have seen that when an outside threat is no longer perceived as a threat, Frank easily re-evaluates it. But when the threat originates from the inside, Frank often continues to send negative cognitions, e.g., "Oh, no!" "You can't handle this," signals to Amy even when there is no real danger. Such messages work well to *stop* us from pursuing our goals in life. These messages block us from thinking clearly and from seeing realistic options.

As babies, our brains began the process of "hardwiring" our responses. Once a reaction is firmly established, we often react automatically. The limbic system responds much faster than the slower deliberation of the cortex. The more trauma in the past, the more Frank may need outside help to assess the situation and calm.

Another challenge is that even after Frank gives an all-clear message, Pete and Andy, the pituitary and adrenal glands, who aroused the entire sympathetic nervous system, did a good job of "spraying" chemicals everywhere. And, as long as they continue doing so, like in a vicious circle, Frank won't be able to stop Amy's upset.

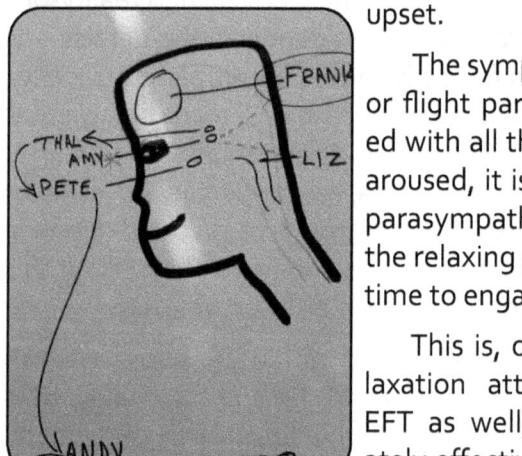

The sympathetic system, the fight or flight part of our body, is activated with all those chemicals, and once aroused, it is slow to back down. The parasympathetic nervous system—the relaxing part—also takes its sweet time to engage.

This is, of course, why typical relaxation attempts, and sometimes EFT as well, aren't always immediately effective. And with chronic high arousal in the body, the client will need additional tools, encouragement, and practice to be able to evaluate the reality of the danger. In addition to education, the client needs empathy, encouragement, longer processing time, and reinforcement for practicing new skills.

Fortunately, while we don't know the exact "something" that happens with EFT, tapping most often results in calming the body and resolving chronic reactions to "false" messages. Our body calms. We can "think more clearly about our problem." We can explore and practice other ways of reacting. We gain more sense of self-control and empowerment.

NOTES

Because we often grasp things better visually, in a face-to-face session, I accompany variations of this story with a rough drawing. *Rough* is the operative word here! I am not in the group of people who have significantly "more grey matter in an area of the brain called the precuneus in the parietal lobe." We call them Artists.* <smile>

P.S. Many readers wrote that they printed this article for their clients. You can find a client-friendly version at https://FromtheDeskofAnnAdams.com

Credit: Image by author

*Quote from http://www.bbc.com/news/science-environment-26925271

13

How Veterans Perceive Therapy and Therapists

IN A NUTSHELL: Bellaruth Naparstek, well-known in the trauma field for her work with Guided Imagery, gave a talk at NICABM* in 2011, sharing her experiences working with veterans for a year at Fort Sill in Oklahoma. She stated that only 50% of veterans with distress ever come for services. Of the half that do walk into the "Behavioral Health" services door, you have only about 20 minutes to show them you "get them" before 60% decide to drop out after the first visit. This article represents the highlights of her presentation.

Her numbers equate to about 70% of veterans with distress not receiving mental health services! While her data is from conventional mental health programs and does not include those seeking EFT services, we still can learn from this information. What are the barriers we could overcome? *What does it take to engage the veteran effectively?*

Surprisingly, the stigma of going for mental health services is *not* the largest barrier to services. An even greater issue was that veterans have *significant levels of "distrust, dislike, and contempt"* for providers. *What can we, as EFT practitioners, do to be perceived differently?*

EFT IS SIMPLE—PEOPLE ARE COMPLEX

Naparstek stressed several points in working with veterans:

- It's about the mission, the team. It is not "all about me," where we practitioners often encourage clients to focus.

- It's about action, not about feelings.

- Humility and understatement are expected. Go watch Gary Cooper in the movie *High Noon* for an example of what they respect.

- Be more formal in addressing officers—call him or her, "sir." Enlisted men may be OK with informality, slang, and profanity.

- Flexibility and speed are respected. They are used to "changing on a dime." Mulling, pondering, obsessing, they see as contemptible.

- Say what you mean, get to the point, then shut up, no embellishments.

- They take their "lumps" with no whining or excuses—we do occasionally encourage people to "whine" to "let it all out." Don't.

- Be gracious, give credit to others, take the blame.

- The brotherhood, or sisterhood, is its own planet. Civilians don't understand.

- Use their preferred terminology. Use "situational awareness" instead of hypervigilance, "combat stress" instead of PTS or Post Traumatic Stress.

Adding the term "Disorder" to PTS, making it PTSD, is an even worse choice of words. Using the term PTSD makes them feel judged and a "nut case." Combat stress is more meaningful and acceptable terminology.

You have a definite disadvantage, in their perception, of your ability to help if you do not have military experience. Deal with this upfront. Admit it. Give a message of, *"It's a disadvantage to* both of us that I don't have the same background of military service. Be patient with me and help me understand. You can teach me as we go."

Do's and Don'ts for Therapists of Veterans

During her year at Ft. Sill, Naparstek asked numerous veterans what the "worst" and "best" things were that therapists had ever done. Their responses create a list of what-to-do and what-*not*-to-do when working with a veteran.

Some of this list may feel like Counseling 101. Much of this list we should already respectfully do or not do for everyone. Keep in mind, however, that these therapist behaviors are on the list because either *doing it was very important or not doing it tended to cut rapport* or send the veteran out the door.

- ▶ LISTEN! Patiently. Let them tell their story. Use their words.
- ▶ Don't expect them to spill their guts in the first session. The quality of your listening, your attitude of respect, and your level of interest affect rapport—and a second visit.
- ▶ Make eye contact.
- ▶ Be authentic. Do not try to fake it. Do not hide behind your status or position.
- ▶ If you do have military medals, certifications, etc., display them.
- ▶ Get out from behind your desk. Be comfortable, relaxed.
- ▶ Add a psycho-educational component. Explain the brain science to help them understand why they have the reactions they do.
- ▶ Don't abruptly end the session. Leave time for a meaningful transition to the end.
- ▶ Don't compare combat trauma with civilian trauma.

- ▶ Don't ask if they've killed anyone.
- ▶ Don't be in a hurry to start, or refer, for medication. Listen first.
- ▶ Don't bring your politics into the session—pro or con.
- ▶ Don't ask about their childhood history. *There is enough to deal with in the here and now.* It is OK to address if the veteran brings it up.
- ▶ Don't give false assurances. They can master the symptoms and can grow from the experience. They can come out of it stronger, but they will never go back to being the "same" as before.
- ▶ Never say that you "understand."

Naparstek agrees with many trauma experts who say that traditional talk therapy is not effective for PTS or PTSD. She recommends that all therapists become proficient in two or three alternative techniques and included EFT on her recommended list. She encourages therapists to develop a network of referral sources for other alternatives.

Take the time as well to ask yourself if you are the right person or if you should refer. Gary Craig's injunction of "don't go where you don't belong" fits here. It is good to have a team of other practitioners to whom you can refer.

> **There is no shame or sense of failure in recognizing when you are not the best person for someone.**

NOTES

Credit:

Bellaruth Naparstek website: https://www.healthjourneys.com/

* NICABM – An educational organization offering continuing education credits for therapists. Open to anyone wishing to increase their knowledge of working with others. An excellent resource. https://nicabm.com

14

Constricted Breathing

> **IN A NUTSHELL:** The EFT breathing exercise is generally taught in classes as an introductory exercise, afterward perhaps briefly mentioned. That's unfortunate. The Constricted Breathing exercise is powerful—all by itself. It is a subtle, gentle, adaptable, useful technique for a variety of situations. Even with all its benefits, Constricted Breathing Exercise is probably the most underutilized of the EFT techniques.

The Constricted Breathing Exercise has many uses:

- Introducing EFT and creating a bridge,
- Calming the client, *at the beginning* of a session and *any point during* a session,
- Creating and deepening rapport and sense of safety,
- Helping to assess client readiness, willingness, and ability to use EFT,
- A fallback when the session gets complex, and intensity begins to rise,
- Or the client needs to slow down,

- And as an assignment—tapping and breathing is a simple use of EFT.

Introducing EFT – We utilize points on our body that *are already familiar* to everyone. We rub around our eyes; we put our hands to our chest; we place our hands under our arm; we scratch our head; we put our head in our hands, etc. Breathing is also a familiar concept! Combining breathing with tapping as someone's introduction to EFT is a simple, easy bridge. Using words is optional, and the exercise almost always generates calm.

Calming – Our emotions show up in our bodies—and our breath. Tapping for a constricted breath decreases anxiety and *sets up the body to ease into any presented issue.*

Safety and rapport – Tapping for the breath is a neutral place to start a session. The client has *a positive experience of calming while using EFT* without focusing on any of their "scary stuff." They immediately see that tapping can be helpful even if their breath does not increase to 100%.

Assessment – Tapping first for the breath gives you a strong indicator of their level of body awareness and their ability to self-regulate their emotions. The breathing exercise can begin the process of *developing and increasing body awareness*, particularly in those out of touch with their body. You can note, too, how well they are *willing to use, and able to respond to, EFT.* You will be *assessing and increasing the depth of rapport* as well.

Back-up – Sometimes clients—and we as practitioners—may get stuck, or the session seems to be going in circles, or you're just not sure what's going on, or things are getting too heavy, etc. It happens. Take a break to simply breathe and tap for the level of the breath. As you are tapping *to increase the depth of the breath, at the same time you are decreasing the intensity* of the fear, anxiety, confusion, etc., that the client is feeling.

Following with the question, *"What comes up for you now?"* often seems to break the stuck cycle, give a fresh start, and a better idea as to what's going on or where to go next.

As an Assignment – Your clients happily complete all assign-

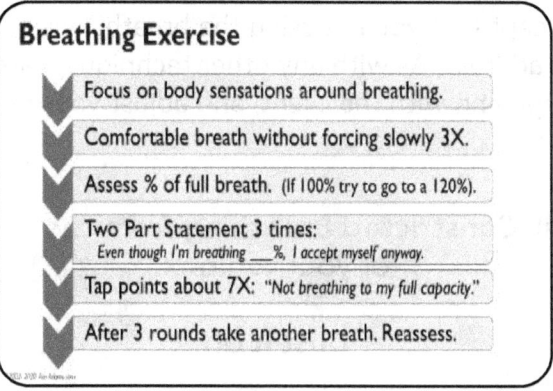

ments you suggest for them—right? Just kidding! Compliance with homework is an issue, no matter your modality or skill level. Compliance is increased when instructions are simple, *"When you are feeling any upset, stop to focus on the depth of your breathing. Tap whatever points you remember until you are calm. You don't have to use any words; you don't have to worry about what to say."* I do give other homework, depending on the issue. However, when I've asked clients after several sessions what "tool" I've shared is most helpful, it's not unusual to hear, "Tapping and breathing."

People are *not always clear about what is bothering them*. Fortunately, we don't have to know the underlying factors to begin calming ourselves. We don't have to figure out what to focus on when tapping. We don't have to think about the details or words. The *higher the emotion, the less the cognitive brain functions*. Keeping the instructions and process simple, especially at first, makes using EFT easier and more acceptable.

Most of us were briefly introduced to the Constricted Breathing Exercise in an EFT class to demonstrate the EFT points and practice using EFT. Constricted Breathing may be then forgotten amid all the other EFT techniques. We often miss the opportunity to explore the power and variety of Constricted Breathing as a meaningful option. It can be a very gentle way to introduce EFT and to ease into difficult issues. Sometimes clients will have a memory or emotion come up. Asking them about their experience may give you the next piece to address.

Exploring the depth and quality of one's breath is like Chasing the Pain except that you are using the breath as the "pain" to focus on and address. As with any other technique, carefully watch what is happening with the client, and adjust your responses and techniques appropriately.

> **Pull Constricted Breathing from the back of your toolbox.**
>
> **Dust it off.**
>
> **It is a powerful tool.**
>
> **Use it!**

Instructions for Constricted Breathing

- ▶ Take three slow comfortable breaths, don't force it.

- ▶ Assess the level of constriction in your current breath as compared to a truly full breath. I like to use percentages, but the 0 to 10 scale works as well.
  "What percentage did you take of a full deep breath?"
  If it's 100% ask them to try to go to 120%.

- ▶ Develop a Setup such as:
  "Even though I'm breathing at [X] %, I deeply and completely accept myself."
  "Even though I am not breathing to my full capacity, I accept myself anyway."

- ▶ Tap the points with no words or using Reminder Phrases such as,
  "Not breathing to my full capacity." "Only breathing at X %." "Not taking a full breath."

- ▶ Tap around the points several times. I lead a client through three rounds before testing again.

CONSTRICTED BREATHING

▶ Take another full breath and reassess %.

▶ If not 100%, repeat a couple of times.

NOTES

Credit: Sample Slide modified from EFT4PowerPoint version 3020
https://www.eft4powerpoint.com

15

Changing Addictive Behavior

> **IN A NUTSHELL:** Learning to recognize early warning signs of a problem is the first step to meaningful change. *Awareness and the ability to shift to an alternative behavior is critical to developing any new habit.* This process may take detective work, multiple visits, and lots of support. While *working with serious addiction requires additional training* beyond EFT, the ideas below offered by Sue Beer and Gwyneth Moss, both EFT Founding Masters in the UK, can be useful for any unwanted behavior.

Sue Beer has worked with addictions for many years. She lists three important factors:

- the **context** in which the behavior occurs,
- the **purpose** it serves, and
- the importance of giving an **alternative**.

The Context – There is always a *context*, internal or external, within which the problem behavior or pattern takes place: a place, a person, a mood, a thought, a particular time. Addictive behavior can appear to *just happen*, like we were on autopilot, seemingly against our normal will. A first step challenging this assumption is to become aware of the context.

Start with these questions:

- **What exactly are you doing?**
- **Where are you?**
- **When does the behavior most happen?**
- **Who with?**
- **What for?**
- **What happens afterward?**

> **Addictive Behavior is an attempt at a solution.**

Creating increased awareness of the context gives information about our thoughts, feelings, and physical sensations useful for Setup wording.

- *Even though [this] always happens [when I'm with Lucy], I accept myself anyway.*
- *Even though [this] is somehow connected with the strange feeling in the pit of my stomach, ...*
- *Even though I have to [eat ice cream, have a drink,] ...*

The Purpose — Addiction, and almost all habitual behavior, has a purpose. When we are beyond our threshold to cope, the *addictive behavior is an attempt at a solution to the pain* of thoughts such as I am not ok/safe/valuable/loveable/confident enough... The substance or behavior we use represents our hope for a solution. The solution becomes temporarily disconnected from the negative consequences we experience afterward. We have to temporarily forget, or we wouldn't be able to do the addictive thing again!

Creating *increased awareness of our body's sensations at the start of the unwanted feelings* that lead to problematic behavior(s) can take the behavior off autopilot. Think of your favorite problem behavior and fill in the blanks:

- I have to... *(what?)*

CHANGING ADDICTIVE BEHAVIOR

- to... *(feel/be/have what?)*
- and then I [what happens – *the negative consequence.*]

For example, a binge drinker might respond:

- *I have to [drink]*
- *to [feel confident socially] ...*
- *and what happens then is [I feel guilt and remorse].*

The Alternative – A client needs to know they have an *alternative*, another choice to use whenever the feeling occurs that leads to the problem behavior. EFT is a powerful alternative when used as soon as the unwanted feelings are noticed. EFT can also help you learn to recognize, and act on, those early warning signs.

Develop a simple, even generic, Setup initially when you first recognize the beginning of the negative initiating feeling. A Setup can be as simple as, *even though I have this craving (or anxiety/fear/ irritation) ... I deeply and completely accept myself.* Addressing the context, purpose and alternatives, will make a significant difference in changing any addictive behavior.

Gwyneth Moss also gives suggestions for addressing cravings and other habitual behaviors.

▶ Start with, *"What is it like when you want to do it?"* The feeling of wanting to do it, the action of doing it, the relief of doing it. Tap through all of that in tiny, tiny, specific detail.

▶ Next, *"What makes you want to do it?"* Where are you, what is going on, who are you with, what is happening, tap through all of that also in tiny, specific detail. Look for patterns, look for Tell the Story opportunities, tap through it all.

▶ Next, *"What was happening in your life around the time this habit started? What was stressful then? What changed then?"* Tap through Movies and Stories. Look for patterns and issues. *Look for the stuff behind the stuff.* Again, tap through in tiny, tiny detail.

▶ Keep coming back to where you started. Notice what has changed. Practice situations that would previously have set off the behavior. Do you still want/need to do it?

NOTES

To change any behavior, you must *first become aware of the body sensations or feelings drawing you toward the behavior before you can utilize a different alternative.* As Carol Look, EFT Master in New York City, is fond of saying, "You don't tap when you are on the way to the donut store."

Sue Beer is one of four addiction experts who participated in the useful EFT set: *Healing the Cycle of Addiction* – a nine-hour mini-course reviewing the factors behind addictions of all sorts. She was joined by EFT Founding Masters, Carol Look, David Rourke, and Loretta Sparks. https://EFTMasterTraining.com

"I love the Healing the Cycle of Addiction CDs. I've worked in chemical dependency for 25 years, and it's like a total refresher course. I watch them at lunch often. A perfect way to relax and learn. Thank you so much." - Debra Angarola, LCSW

Whether you are an expert or a beginner, you will find this set useful in working with any habit, craving, or addictive behavior. https://www.eftforaddiction.com/

Credits:

Sue Beer: [https://theEFTCentre.com] Sue Beer's section edited from her article in the EFT Masters World Wide Newsletter 2008.

Gwyneth Moss comments are from email to EFTGuild: https://efthelps.com/

16

Individualizing Affirmations

IN A NUTSHELL: Making the positive statement, "I deeply and completely accept myself" can be difficult for some clients to say, much less accept. Instructing the client to, "Just say it," could miss an opportunity to empower a client who already feels out of control of their life.

Practitioners are taught to "use the client's words" as we tap. We listen carefully and develop Setups that reflect the client's issue. We check if the Setup resonates. We don't, however, always give the same consideration in using client words in creating the positive side of the Setup.

Clients may come in feeling like a victim, believing they have no power, no resources, and little or no control in their lives. Most come with low self-esteem in some part, if not all, of their life, little confidence, and high anxiety. They have lots of negative self-talk about their worth and little faith in their competence. *When we are upset, we tend to skip positive thoughts about ourselves.* A personalized affirmation a client can accept that highlights a current strength and ability, particularly when they don't feel they have much or any, increases confidence and competence.

We may explain the Setup is not tapping on the "negative" but is a reflection of their "truth" in this present moment. Practitioners may miss that the client's "truth" in the present moment is *not a positive thought about acceptance of self*—or that they love, honor, trust, respect, etc., themselves either.

Working with the client to help them discover what *is true* for them, *right now* at this moment, can be the first step toward self-acceptance. Positive statements, created with the client's words, can be more effective and more empowering than the "just say it" injunction. As Pat Carrington* often said, "It's hard to argue with your own words."

Explore with the client what they may recognize, perhaps for the first time, what they *do find acceptable* about themselves. A few minutes conversation can yield a variety of individualized Set-ups with words the client is comfortable using immediately—their own meaningful, unique, positive statement.

There are many alternatives to the default. Whatever they *can* accept about themselves will work. They might need a suggestion. One option would be to tap for, "Even though I cannot think of even one thing positive about myself," then add a strength *you* identified that the client has? Add waffle words: I'll *think* about, *maybe*, accepting myself *someday maybe.* Or recognize the strength it took to make the appointment: "I found the courage to try EFT."

Within a Setup, the words of the positive statement are not important. What *is* important is that it is *their words*. What *is* true for that client, right now, despite the problem? Making a statement feel is true begins reframing their view of self.

When the client has trouble finding *anything* positive, point out an obvious concrete strength, or behavior you've noticed, a kind act or words of encouragement that they didn't recognize within themselves.

INDIVIDUALIZING AFFIRMATIONS

It doesn't matter how minor that positive statement is.

It's ok to give them suggestions:

...A least I've taken the first step by making this appointment.

...I keep going in spite of it all.

...I do have the strength to keep the appointment I made.

...I have the good judgment to begin the process of finding resources to help me.

...I can give myself credit for trying something new to deal with this.

...I got up, I got dressed, I decided to take action, and I'm here.

...I have a problem I don't know how to solve, yet, but I dared to seek help.

...I admire my persistence for keeping on trying to find an answer.

...I do have control of how slow or fast and what we discuss.

...I choose what I want to share and what I don't.

...My children love me.

...My dog thinks I'm terrific.

...My cat loves me. [Sometimes adding slight humor is helpful.]

...I make great brownies.

...I keep on keeping on, I haven't given up even though I wanted to.

"Waffle" words may be necessary to begin creating hope for the future.

...I want to (or would like to) accept myself.

...I'll think about accepting myself, someday, maybe.

...There's something, somewhere to accept about myself.

...I can accept myself right now at this moment for at least the next 30 seconds.

Don't tell them to, "Just say it." Don't let your client miss the opportunity to have the experience to recognize, and own, what is positive. This practice is also helpful in building rapport and sneaking up toward a problem. Help your client create a Setup that they feel is true for them in the moment and take steps toward more empowerment.

NOTES

Credits:
*Patricia Carrington Ph.D. was a leader in the EFT world and developed the Choice Method. She died in October 2019, at age 95, still working to share her EFT knowledge. Her website continues to shares useful information.

Drawing of two women by Kari Reed Tumminia, an artist, EFT coach, and author of "No Bad Dates" http://www.ktumminia.com/

17

EFT and Dreams

> **IN A NUTSHELL:** Ever woke from a dream and wondered: What was *that* all about? Here is a useful and fun alternative toward figuring out what, indeed, the dream was about.

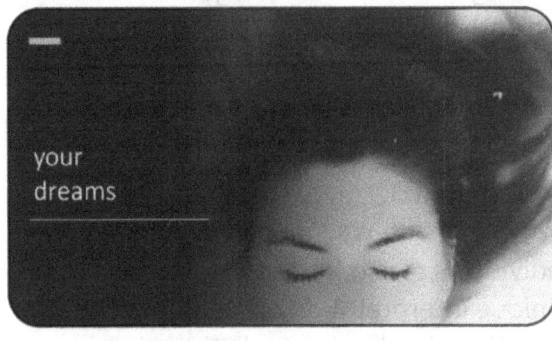

In graduate school, I learned Fritz Perl's and Carl Jung's theories on working with dreams. They thought that every image in a dream is a broken off part of your personality. Jung believed that *dreams focus on the most important unfinished business of the day and can put us in touch with our often subconscious with personal issues.*

I was taught to have the client role-play each piece of the dream and assist them in gaining meaning from the associations to their waking life. The concept is interesting and insightful, but as is often the case, in practice, merely gaining insight is frequently not enough to change behavior.

Bob and Lynn Hoss have been studying dreams for many

years. At an ACEP Conference presentation, they shared a useful format for using EFT to find the associations with your waking life in your dreams. In the *Image Activation Technique*, you identify the most compelling image in your dream, then imagine *you are that image* and answer six questions *as if you were the image.* Next, use your answers to lead to a current stressful issue to address using EFT.

Addressing a dream image can quickly assist in helping find the top priority for an energy session. *The theory is that dreaming represents images that are the non-literal representations of our emotions.*

Bob Hoss gave the example of "Joan's" dream. She was being examined in a health clinic. The nurse told her, "You are 'riddled' with cancer." Joan said that in the dream, she was not afraid of dying but wanted something to prevent the pain. She woke up concerned, and, like most of us if we had such a dream, did go to the doctor. She did not have cancer. In an earlier session, she had shared that she had a strong interest in astrology. She drew the parallel that she was currently "puzzling," i.e., the riddle, on how to break up with her boyfriend who had the zodiac sign of Cancer. Her challenge was how to dissolve the relationship without the usual emotional pain that comes with most relationship breakups.

Look at the door of your room. Think of the multiple functions of the door: a passageway, way out, way in, barrier, privacy, connection, opportunity. Individuals give different associations to objects in their dream, a unique interpretation or meaning. The variety of individual interpretations is why dream dictionaries are not useful—each person may have a different interpretation for the dream image. In using the *Image Activation Technique*, we ask the image, i.e., our subconscious, for the interpretation.

Image Activation Technique Steps

Step 1: Identify a dream. Write down your dream immediately upon awakening. This may take a bit of practice.

Step 2: Run through the dream story quickly.

EFT AND DREAMS

Pick the most compelling image in your dream; the *one* image that seems the most important, no matter how small a part it plays. Take a few slow breaths, *imagine yourself as that image*. Then **answer the questions below, as that image,** use the first person "I." If you have a challenge "being" your most compelling image, simply *guess* what you think it *might* say. In other words, make it up.

Step 3: Answer *as* your most compelling image. Write down the answers.

a. What are you?

I am _____

b. What is your purpose?

My purpose is _____

c. What do you like about being this thing in the dream?

I like _____

d. What do you dislike about being this thing in the dream?

I dislike _____

e. What do you fear most?

I am most afraid of _____

f. What do you desire most?

What I most desire is _____

Step 4: Do any of the answers remind you of a recent situation or feeling in your waking life?

Back to being you. These answers often relate to a problem situation in your waking life. Go through each answer gleaned from your image.

Step 5: How does this answer relate to your current problem?

Look for a specific scene or incident to address with EFT. Look for one that either resonates the most, is the most emotionally impacting, or best recalls or relates to the waking life situation. Perhaps asking yourself **when, in your waking life, have you *felt*** *the way you felt in the dream* could lead you to a specific incident.

Step 6: Create an EFT Setup – the problem/acceptance statement.

When applicable, use what the image *liked or desired most* as part of the acceptance statement. For example, you liked that you were brave; what you most desired was to be calm and confident. The acceptance statement could then be, I choose to be brave, calm, and confident.

Step 7: Use EFT to reduce the stress as much as you can from that one incident before you move to another. Continue rounds of EFT until the stress is negated or reduced. You could use our favorite global default question: What comes up now?

Step 8: Go back into the dream; ask the questions again; observe what's happening. At the end of the dream—*using whatever pops into your mind*—**give the dream a new ending that works for everybody/everything in the dream.** It can be a totally "wild and crazy" metaphor or interpretation or a clear solution. However, any answer needs to pass the test:

- **Is it practical?**
- **Is it appropriate?**
- **Does it allow you to progress in life, i.e., not set you back?**

Step 9: Turn your new learning into actions, something useful in real life. Define the next steps to create a plan of action including *how and when* you will put it into practice.

Step 10: Identify a reminder phrase or token that relates in some way to the key image in your dream.

Go try it! It's a fun and interesting twist on using EFT.

NOTES

Credits:
Learn more about working with dreams: http://www.dreamscience.org
The dream photo by Glen Hodson on Unsplash.com was modified in PowerPoint.

18

How Do Innovations Spread?

> **IN A NUTSHELL:** When we learn about, then benefit from, EFT, we want to enthusiastically share this amazing tool. We are a bit hurt or miffed or just puzzled that not everyone embraces tapping on spots of your body to reduce emotional turmoil! We wonder why everyone would not jump at such a safe, easy, effective method. Why doesn't your family? Why wouldn't every hospital, VA program, school system, etc. embrace such a useful technique?

I asked readers to share their experiences when they introduced EFT to their family. One reader replied, "I've just backed off. They don't want to hear about it from me. When they do turn their opinion around, it is because they hear it from someone else. That's okay with me. I planted the seed." How wise. How respectful. How aware. Realistically, it's pretty hard to successfully "push" your agenda on others anyway.

The Diffusion of Innovations by Everett Rogers, states that pretty much every new idea goes through a process to spread among a given population. Naturally, some innovations are "diffused" faster than others, and some never make it to the tipping point of acceptance by the majority of the population.

Someone comes up with a new idea—the "Innovator." The innovator introduces the idea to others; the first people to accept the new idea are called "Early Adopters." Many of you are either Early Adopters of EFT or belong to the next group to adopt the idea, the "Early Majority." Unfortunately, it is not the Innovator or Early Adopters or Early Majority, who take any idea to the "tipping point" in the population.

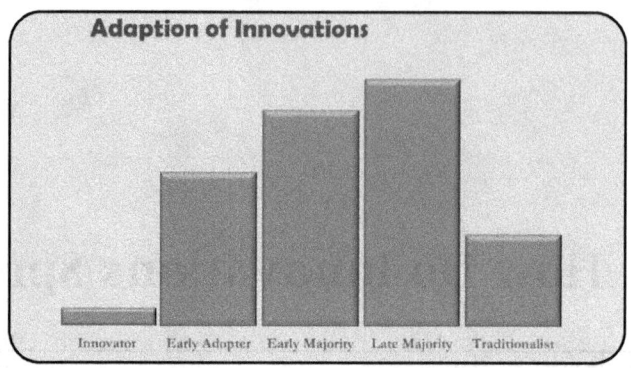

The bar graph gives a visual of this concept. Here's how it works. The people who find the idea beneficial in some way, the **Early Adopters**, use it and introduce it to others, some of whom, the **Early Majority**, accept and use the innovation. The Early Majority users begin to grow in numbers sufficient to be visible to others. They influence others, the **Late Majority**. As the innovation gains enough "social proof" to perhaps be a useful/safe/acceptable idea and the idea is headed toward the tipping point.

The **Traditionalists,** sometimes called laggards, respond only when there are already large numbers of people accepting and/or using the concept. These numbers would include the Late Majority, the Early Majority, and Early Adopters.

This need by the Traditionalist for a majority of people to accept the idea is a challenge to us Early Adopters. We want so badly for *everyone* to see how beneficial EFT can be. We often see the Traditionalists as *the* key to that broad spread acceptance. The reality is that the Traditionalists *are often not the major influencer.* While individually the Traditionalist may be personally in favor of the innovation, many others must adopt it, in most cases, before Traditionalists feel safe enough to publicly endorse it. Even changes that appear to happen from the "top-down" rarely succeed unless there is a majority of support garnered from below.

Accelerating Acceptance – This process can be accelerated when those people who hold the formal or informal positions of influence with credibility and "social capital" among their "followers" see the idea as helpful. In the same way, these people of influence can also stop an innovation. For example, the acceptance of vaccines for childhood diseases among indigenous people was increased in communities when a person in their community, in a formal or informal position of influence, is seen as credible by the majority of the group approved of the innovation. When that person of influence did not see it as credible, the acceptance level by the group was low.

Communication Challenges – As you move up the bar graph toward adoption, the level of interpersonal influence increases. The more respect and credibility and people the "leader" influence, the faster it is accepted. And not necessarily formal leaders, often those informal "mavens" who seem to know everyone and are seen as experienced and knowledgeable and trusted by others are the key influencers.

A challenge to the spread of an innovative idea is that, typically, the diffusion groups are only able to communicate in a credible way to one level up and one level down. This means the innovator directly influences the Early Adopters; the Early Adopters influence the Early Majority who have little or no direct access to the innovator. The Early Majority then influences the Late Majority; the Late Majority influences the holdouts, the Traditionalists. It follows that, for the most part, we Early Adopters are *not* going to be the group that carries EFT to those Traditionalists.

This frustrates us Early Adopter and Early Majority folks who really, really want to directly approach the Traditionalists about the benefits of EFT—*now*, not later! Our goal as Early Adopters is *not* to influence nor convince the Traditionalists. Our job is to share with people in our current environment who are most open to the idea. These people then influence others who, either directly or indirectly, will impact the decision-makers, the influencers. Our job is to lay the groundwork, or as the saying goes, plant the seed.

Before adopting any idea, you first need to be aware that an option exists. After awareness of an option, you will need to be "persuaded" in a language you understand, that "bridge" to understanding, to give it a try. Potential adopters often want to know the degree to which a new idea is better than an existing practice. This means stating or showing the benefits of EFT *in a way that is relevant to your audience.*

Traditionalists, like gravity, have an important job as "cultural stabilizers," otherwise we would wake up in a new world every morning with an overwhelming number of changes every day. Indeed, many of us feel stressed and challenged keeping up with all changes happening now. Yes, many cultural things may need changing, but we are not going to change them until there are sufficient others, i.e., the Early and Late Majority, that accept the change.

Still, EFT practitioners want to see EFT accepted *now* by agencies, institutions, schools, the military, and mental health centers, etc. We ask, why, oh why, don't they see how useful, how effective, how inexpensive, how easy? Well, they don't—yet! But you *can* "bloom where you are planted."

> **You can do what you can with whom you can where you can—today.**

You do not have to travel or be active on the internet or establish a big business. You do not have to be a Gary Craig to be able to contribute to the betterment of the world. Every person you introduce to EFT moves it toward acceptance. *Every time you do anything that helps someone feel a bit better about themselves, you have made the world a better place.*

> **Help someone feel better and make the world a better place.**

HOW DO INNOVATIONS SPREAD?

Every person is an influencer in some way. Building trust and relationships take time. *Go slow, build support, be patient.* Take advantage of the opportunities you have, right where you are, with the people and resources available around you. *Bloom where you are planted.*

TRIVIA: Wonder where the "bloom where you are planted" quote originated? The words are *not* in the Bible. The closest quote is Matthew 5:1: "In the same way, let your light shine before others, that they may see your good deeds and glorify your Father in heaven."

Mary Englebreit made the phrase famous in her book, *The Art and the Artist,* and the American radio broadcaster, Paul Harvey used the phrase a decade before Mary's book, but neither was the originator. Most agree that the origin of the statement goes back to the 16th century Bishop of Geneva, Saint Francis de Sales. The bishop is first credited with the statement based on his quote, "Truly charity has no limit; for the love of God has been poured into our hearts by His Spirit dwelling in each one of us, calling us to a life of devotion and inviting us to *bloom in the garden where He has planted* and directing us to radiate the beauty and spread the fragrance of His Providence."*

NOTES

Credits:

Graphics are from EFT4PowerPoint Comprehensive EFT Training Program Resource and EFT4PowerPoint.

*https://bgav.org/bloom-where-youre-planted/

19

EFT is Like Systematic Desensitization

IN A NUTSHELL: Systematic Desensitization (SD), used since the 50s, is a therapeutic technique designed to treat anxiety and phobias. It is similar to EFT as it pairs increasingly intense details of the issue but uses relaxation exercises instead of EFT to help resolve the issue. The SD therapist guides the patient to imagine the upsetting image and then help them switch to a relaxed state over and over as they climb the "ladder" of intense images. SD could be even more powerful and less emotionally upsetting if various EFT techniques were added along the way.

For 26 years in the Georgia state mental health system, I was a therapist, supervisor, and administrator. Then for six years, I was the director of a residential treatment program for children before I retired to become a full-time EFTer. My interest in the energy psychology world was sparked because 1) I was only too aware of the limits in how we could help some clients, and 2) I saw parallels with some "traditional" techniques that I had found to be helpful. SD was one of those.

The drop-out rate for Systematic Desensitization is high. The process is involved, difficult, and can take many sessions and trigger very strong negative reactions. The therapist and patient

make a list, a hierarchy, of increasingly anxiety-producing images from a trauma. Starting with the least upsetting aspect, they address one image at a time. The goal is to become desensitized, to *react in a realistic* way to the image or thing.

For participants who complete the series of steps, there is a high success rate for the resolution of their symptoms. In other words, if you hung in, SD was effective.

Naturally, for the client to be willing to go through this process, strong rapport and a sense of safety must be established.

Using EFT, we tap to assure the emotional arousal is low before addressing memories that may cause high emotion. SD therapists, like experienced EFT practitioners, start with the more minor aspects of the traumatic memory, circling slowly toward the most emotionally laden parts, a type of "sneaking up." EFT works to balance the energy, i.e., like SD generates relaxation, for each piece of the memory before moving on. Skillfully managed, EFT most often avoids the intense adverse reactions common with the use of SD.

You cannot be upset and calm at the same time. The sympathetic or parasympathetic systems have opposite impacts on the body. The goal of SD is to pair the upsetting image and relaxation together until the person realizes they are in a safe environment and the event is no longer a threat to them. EFT also pairs the upset with a calming action—tapping. By addressing the energy system, EFT adds the benefit of being effective faster and with less upset than SD.

Much less triggering of intensity could be prevented *if* EFT was taught to the client as a self-help skill! One of my students worked with veterans in a Navy facility that mandated SD for PTSD patients. While EFT was not an "approved" technique at the time, if the patient became highly emotionally aroused, she led them through tapping or the Touch and Breathe process, i.e., touching each point, instead of tapping it, as you take a slow breath until they became calm enough to continue EFT.

The goals in SD, as in most other therapeutic approaches, are similar to EFT.

- Establish deep rapport to increase the client's willingness to share fearful information, relate memories, and follow the process.

- Create a joint agreement that the process will move only as fast as the client is comfortable, i.e., at the client's pace. Ensures the client feels calm and safe before going to the next step. *Techniques with a tendency to push the client without building readiness and agreement have a higher drop-out rate.*

- Address first how the client feels about *having* the problem and how they feel about addressing it currently, with the practitioner, e.g., the fear, shame, embarrassment, anger, etc. The presenting problem is not addressed until these feelings are neutralized or low.

- Start with a small piece of the upsetting image or issue using a "distancing technique," such as imagining the scene as far away or safely held in some container.

- Identify and tap each intense aspect of the body's feelings and images. Create relaxation in the body before gradually moving up the "ladder" or moving the image closer and more exposed to view.

The client should address all aspects and memories that come up, with intensity of zero, and be able to observe the previously anxiety-producing memory/image/thing without a strong emotional reaction. Sometimes clients have not only conquered the fear but are willing to experience a situation that could bring it on. For example, go into the water, drive across the bridge, pet the snake or mouse, open the door and go outside, etc. An in vivo experience is the ultimate test of results.

EFT takes less time, with less fear, and more satisfaction. Adding EFT to other therapeutic techniques could increase the effectiveness of any method, deepen rapport, decrease resistance more readily, and decrease emotional abreactions.

NOTES

Credit:

Photo by Ethan Johnson on unsplash.com

Research Resource: There is increasing research as to the efficacy of EFT. Find a list of relevant research on the Association of Comprehensive Energy Psychology (ACEP) web site: https://www.energypsych.org/page/Research_Landing

20

Simple and Complex Phobias

> IN A NUTSHELL: A phobia is an extreme, irrational fear of or aversion to something. The person already knows their reaction is irrational, but the emotion overrides the intellect. Phobias may be simple to resolve with EFT when it was created after a single event, or very complex when it is combined with trauma and/or entangled relationships.

There are hundreds of phobias listed on phobialist.com, a minimum of two phobias for every letter in the alphabet except Y. Until EFT, the key treatments for phobias were exposure treatment, (~1986), flooding, counterconditioning (1924), and various forms of systematic desensitization (1958 and later). Phobias were considered difficult to resolve.

For a simple and uncomplicated phobia, identify the event that caused it, clarify the details, and tap for even tiny related aspects, and the fear is often gone. Some phobias, however, that begin as uncomplicated can turn out to be surprisingly complex.

In addition, people can react differently to the same phobia and can be triggered by widely different aspects. An individual can react to one part, many parts, or the entire experience. Flying over land seems OK but flying over water is terrifying. A spider in a book is OK, but even a small spider in a corner is worrisome; if it is

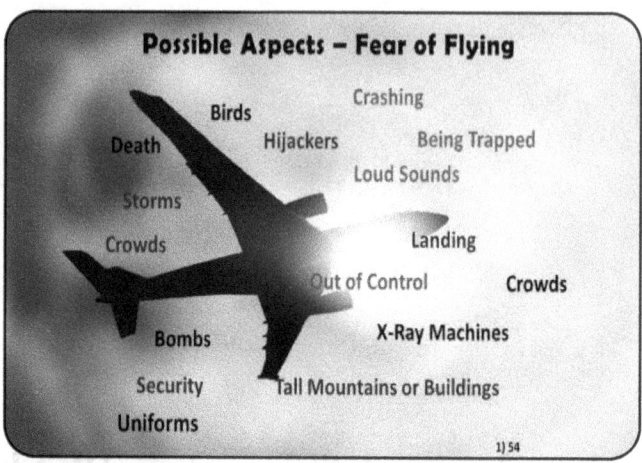

big and moving you run screaming. Snakes in cages may be manageable, but your anxiety goes to 10 when you see a small garden snake in your yard. Even *thinking* about a mouse can bring on a panic attack.

Single Incident Phobia

Cherie is an example of using EFT to resolve a simple phobia. One morning her preschooler wanted her to play with him using Play-Doh. Cherie had an aversion to anything close to what she described as "mushy." She knew her reaction to the mushy Play-Doh would prevent her from enjoying the time with her son.

Cherie was new to tapping and decided to try it on her "mushy" phobia. Beginning with her current physical sensation as she thought of the feel of Play-Doh, she was quickly transported back to an experience when her older brother had put a slug down her back. The intensity of the experience at age eight was still surprisingly high.

The most intense memory was that of his laughing as he was holding her down to put the slug down her back. She tapped several rounds on the sound until, when she looked at the scene again, she could *see* him laughing but could no longer *hear* him laughing.

Cherie tapped for the hurt and disappointment around her brother's behavior. And, while Cherie had known rationally, that she was a little girl and he was older and bigger, with tapping the intellectual realization became reality, "I was just a little girl. He was lots bigger; there was nothing I could do."

NOTE: Most of the reframes we offer, and cognitive shifts clients come to, are not overly brilliant insights. They are most often common sense rational statements: it's over, I survived, he was a sick person, she wanted to protect me and didn't understand she was hurting me, I was just a little girl, that was then this is now, they weren't picking me out, they weren't thinking about me at all, it wasn't my fault, I was in the wrong place at the wrong time, I am angry at my son's behavior because I can't stand the same thing in myself, etc.

When upset, we do not have the highest problem-solving skills, which is 1) why it is important to offer a reframe only after the intensity of the emotion is low, and 2) why the client's cognitive shift is more powerful than any practitioner reframe.

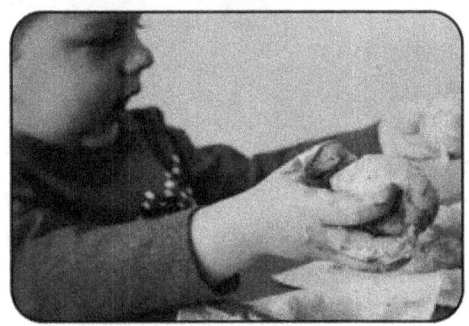

Cherie tapped more rounds on the sadness and hurt that came up; she adored her brother; how could he do such a thing? Then a memory, long forgotten, appeared. Her brother came to tell her good night. He told her he was sorry and promised never to do it again. She had forgotten this part entirely. She now realized he had genuine remorse and shame for what he had done. She replayed the slug scene again. It seemed far away.

She realized that the aversion to "mushy" was symbolic to protect her from disappointment from those she loved and trusted. Cherie smiled to herself as she sat down to happily play with her son *and* the Play-Doh.

Complex Phobias

Phobias tied to one single incident generally respond to addressing within a few EFT sessions, sometimes only one. Phobias that are developed or strengthened by repetitive events, are often tied to complex, tangled, negative, abusive relationships or trauma, can be very complex. Complex phobias may require much more time, lots of support, and a great deal of detective work to resolve.

John's fear of spiders developed as a young child. His father kept a pet tarantula, and, in his misguided attempt to have John share his enthusiasm, frightened him. John was unable to resolve his spider phobia until he worked through many situations in which his father had imposed his will on John without considering or listening to what John wanted or needed.

John's spider phobia was entangled with his image of himself as "not important" and "not worthy of love" and that "what I want doesn't matter." In working with John, the relationship between the two of us was probably as, or even more, important than the tapping—dare I say that! He needed to be truly heard. He needed to have his story and responses carefully considered, his reluctance and resistance respected, his baby steps to self-worth genuinely celebrated.

Any comment I made, I checked with him for his acceptance and thoughts. Only after he realized that what he thought and said mattered, that *he* mattered, did his fear of spiders disappear.

NOTES

Credit: Slide of Airplane phobia modified from EFT4Powerpoint 3020version https://www.eft4powerpoint.com

The child with messy hands photo by Kelly Sikkema on Unsplash

Man Photo by Anastasia Vityukova on Unsplash

21

Muscle Testing

> **IN A NUTSHELL:** In trained and skilled hands, muscle testing can be a useful tool to help assess where to start or where to "go" in a session. Many practitioners find muscle testing helpful and use it frequently. As with any technique, however, there are pros and cons.

WARNING – While I am not opposed unilaterally to muscle testing, and still use it on occasion, this article focuses on the potential downsides of muscle testing. My view may be a "minority position," and some readers may disagree.

The supposition behind muscle testing is that it is a way to get in touch with your subconscious, your higher wisdom. It involves "testing" a muscle as to whether it holds strong or releases under minimal pressure. There are many muscles you could use, but the arm muscles seem to be the most popular.

Muscle testing can demonstrate how negative and positive thoughts impact our bodies. It can quickly *identify a meaningful direction for a session or break an impasse when stuck.* After all, whatever is brought up by the client is related to their issues.

Muscle testing is not a crystal ball able to tell you the future. Should I do this or that questions do not gain clear answers. Don't ask, should I leave my husband? Or should I change jobs? Don't ask anything that is not "yours." Don't ask questions about the future. The question, if I buy this stock will it go up, will not give you any better answer than tossing a coin. Muscle testing can, however, ferret out some of those sneaky little issues from your past that may be involved in why you are considering leaving your husband. We all have conflicts; we all have those "yes but's"—we are complex beings.

Don't ask something your subconscious would not know. While we *may* be all connected in the ultimate universe, and perhaps somewhere there is a universal pool of knowledge that we *could* hypothetically dip into—don't count on it.

I had six full days of muscle testing training and read extensively about it. I took an eight-part course with an alternative practitioner using a pendulum as a critical piece of his work. If I was going to use muscle testing, I wanted to make sure I was good at it! In addition, I watched a couple of dozen successful sessions with practitioners who relied heavily on either muscle testing or a pendulum. I was a client for several sessions as well. I've seen and experienced the benefits of muscle testing. However, even with my training and experience, I rarely use any form of muscle testing in my work with others now. Why?

First, part of my education about muscle testing concerned the ways it could be inaccurate or manipulated by the tester. Humans are fallible beings.

Second, I began to be concerned that muscle testing could bring up "too much, too soon" for some clients. Could muscle testing responses go deeper and/or faster than my client could process on an emotional or cognitive level? To help prevent this, an important question to ask as you are muscle testing would be, *"Is it in your highest and best interest to know the answer to this question now?"*

Third, questions need to be simple yes/no questions about specific details—facts, not suppositions. Is it *this*, or *is it that?* You want a specifically formed question around dates, times, places, things, people. Ask only direct questions for a clear, and hopefully, meaningful answer. Study, detective work, and a lot of practice may be necessary to learn to formulate questions for more accurate answers. Improving accuracy also depends on your ability to "get out of your own way" and being aware of when you *are* not.

Fourth, as I gained experience, I became aware, with uncanny accuracy, of how the muscle would respond as soon as the question was formulated *but* before the client's muscle reacted. I *knew* if the answer was to be a yes or no. Was my intuition expanding? Was I able to recognize an even more subtle response that happened before the muscle noticeably responded? My ego would like to think that. The larger question was, did I in some unconscious way, influence the response of the client? Was I truly, 100% *out of my own way, 100% of the time?* Possible, I suppose, but I doubt it. Experienced or not, I'm still human.

Roger Callahan on Muscle Testing

During Callahan's Thought Field Therapy diagnostic training in 2000, we often broke into dyads to practice using muscle testing to "diagnose" which point needs tapping and in what order. During a Q&A session, I asked Callahan if every person in the room tested the *same* person for the *same* problem *before* any treatment would they get the *same* response as I had. His answer was no. No! He talked about the energetic connection between people and that the energy of the "two" could impact responses. He indicated that the muscle response could be different or could "diagnose" a variation in the order of points, even when different practitioners muscle tested a client on the same issue but before any tapping.

Wow! This was early in my learning about energy psychology, and this was earth-shattering to me. Indeed, this was a key reason I focused primarily on EFT. Gary developed EFT without utilizing muscle testing. However, for many years he still used a form of self muscle testing. He would swing his arm in front of him as a test *for* the client—a longer swing would indicate a yes. Testing *for* the client using any method always needs to be checked with the client to decrease the chances of practitioner bias.

Callahan's comment also drove my decision to take those six

days of muscle testing classes. I wanted to learn to be as objective a tester as possible.

[See chapter on Pendulums and Jugs for examples of detailed questions with the ability to access yes/no factual answers.]

Challenges vs. Benefit

Later, when I read *Power vs. Force* by David Hawkins, I recalled Callahan's remarks and have always wondered how Hawkins trained his assessors to be able to have the exact response with everyone.

- Wouldn't that same level of human energetic connection that Callahan mentioned impact the results?
- Wasn't there a standard deviation of variance? It seems that some natural human variance would be expected.
- What would be a realistic way to assess what, if any, impact the practitioner had on their subject?

In short, I felt there were more challenges than benefits for me, and my client, around muscle testing. Client empowerment ranks high as a value for me as a social worker. I believe in the resilience of humans. I believe *everyone has their own path, their own journey, their own timing.** Muscle testing can shift any of those—and possibly not always in the client's best interest.

Perhaps a fifth reason in the above list is that not every technique is for everyone—client or practitioner. Although on occasion, I do still use muscle testing, it just doesn't fit my core value of self-empowerment or add to the rapport I work to build with my client.

If you do want to use muscle testing, however, as part of your practice, work with someone skilled in using it. The ability to get out of your own way and ask a series of detailed questions for a meaningful response takes time and practice to become proficient.

Tidbit of Trivia: I was at Roger's TFT week-long Level B diagnostic workshop during his 75th birthday, and we were all treated to an awesome, and obviously memorable, carrot cake.

Credit: *An Annism

22

Experiencing Grief

> **IN A NUTSHELL:** The response, below my comments, comes from a Reddit post years ago to a man who had just lost his brother and said he didn't know what to do with his grief. While the post is *not* about EFT, it is an excellent heartfelt description of the experience of grief and offers a normalizing perspective and reframing opportunities when using EFT.

Each client's uniqueness makes it important to go slowly enough to deeply know the person who is sitting in front of you—what is their path, their journey, their timing. Dealing with any trauma can be tricky and potentially retraumatizing. Trauma can be cumulative and surprisingly complex. Trauma can be hidden. Addressing what initially seems to be a minor event can activate a long-buried intense emotion.

> **We have our own path, our own journey, our own timing.***

Then, too, because EFT can often collapse something quickly, we gamble moving ahead of our client, beyond their readiness to "go there." *Because we can does not mean we should.*

We may feel like the session was highly successful but going faster than our client can process. As one responder to the email put it, "I wasn't ready to just be over it; this happened too quickly. I needed more time." Another client stopped when the intensity was a two, saying he didn't want it to go to zero. Sometimes we need the time to honor our feelings, to honor our loved one, to honor our journey.

While tapping can help decrease the pain and increase the times of peace and open the heart to a new type of relationship with those who've left this world, there is still that occasional wave of grief, of the loss. EFT can reduce the size, intensity, and frequency of the waves, help reframe those waves and the scars. perhaps reduce the waves to an occasional gentle one. It can help us accept the loss and develop that new relationship with the person you lost. However, experiencing sadness that our loved one is no longer with us *is* a normal emotion. The below response from an old gentleman resonates with many who have experienced multiple losses, including myself.

Dealing with Grief

I'm old. What that means is that I've survived (so far), and a lot of people I've known and loved did not.

I've lost friends, best friends, acquaintances, co-workers, grandparents, mom, relatives, teachers, mentors, students, neighbors, and a host of other folks. I have no children, and I can't imagine the pain it must be to lose a child. But here's my two cents...

I wish I could say you get used to people dying. *But I never did. I don't want to. It tears a hole through me whenever somebody I love dies, no matter the circumstances. But I don't want it to "not matter." I don't want it to be something that just passes. My scars are a testament to the love and the relationship that I had for and with that person. And if the scar is deep, so was the love. So be it.*

Scars are a testament to life. Scars are a testament that I can love deeply and live deeply and be cut, or even gouged, and that I can heal and continue to live and continue to love. And the scar tis-

EXPERIENCING GRIEF

sue is stronger than the original flesh ever was. Scars are a testament to life. Scars are only ugly to people who can't see.

As for grief, you'll find it comes in waves. When the ship is first wrecked, you're drowning, with wreckage all around you. Everything floating around you reminds you of the beauty and the magnificence of the ship that was and is no more. And all you can do is float. You find some piece of the wreckage, and you hang on for a while. Maybe it's some physical thing. Maybe it's a happy memory or a photograph. Maybe it's a person who is also floating. For a while, all you can do is float. Stay alive.

In the beginning, the waves are 100 feet tall and crash over you without mercy. They come 10 seconds apart and don't even give you time to catch your breath. All you can do is hang on and float. After a while, maybe weeks, maybe months, you'll find the waves are still 100 feet tall, but they come further apart. When they come, they still crash all over you and wipe you out. But in between, you can breathe, you can function. You never know what's going to trigger the grief. It might be a song, a picture, a street intersection, the smell of a cup of coffee. It can be just about anything... and the wave comes crashing. But in between waves, there is life.

Somewhere down the line, and it's different for everybody, you find that the waves are only 80 feet tall. Or 50 feet tall. And while they still come, they come further apart. You can see them coming.

EFT IS SIMPLE—PEOPLE ARE COMPLEX

An anniversary, a birthday, or Christmas, or landing at O'Hare. You can see it coming, for the most part, and prepare yourself. And when it washes over you, you know that somehow you will, again, come out the other side. Soaking wet, sputtering, still hanging on to some tiny piece of the wreckage, but you'll come out.

Take it from an old guy. The waves never stop coming, and somehow you don't really want them to. But you learn that you'll survive them. And other waves will come. And you'll survive them too.

If you're lucky, you'll have lots of scars from lots of loves. And lots of shipwrecks.

NOTES

Credit:

Thanks to Reddit user GSnow.

Wave photo from Unsplash by Joel Mott

23

Tapping Does the Work

> **IN A NUTSHELL:** Basically, the tapping does the work. Tapping activates the acupressure points to do that "something" to balance the energy system and calm our body's responses. Which begs the questions: Do we need words? Do we need a Setup?

Roger Callahan, the developer of Thought Field Therapy (TFT) from whence EFT was spawned, stopped using any words when tapping. As the client focused on their issue, TFT practitioners "diagnose" the order of points to be tapped. In addition, Callahan felt a Setup was necessary only 40% of the time.

In the development of EFT, Gary Craig kept the use of words. However, he stated that words were only 10% of the results; he did not say how he came to that exact percentage. I attended 13 of his live workshops. I watched as occasionally he tapped quietly on his client using no words, and I watched as the client, and the audience, benefited. Most of us have experienced, either by ourselves or with others, having results while tapping with no words.

If we operate on the above assumptions about the "need" for a Setup or words, it appears we could leave out the Setup 60% of the time and words 90% of the time! Should we? Let's look at the pros and cons.

The two-part EFT Setup was designed to "set up," or prepare, the energy system to be responsive to the tapping. Callahan found through his muscle testing that some people were "reversed" in that they tested positive to a negative statement, or negative to a positive statement. When that was the case, tapping was either less effective or not effective at all. A lot has been written about reversals. Some energy practitioners feel identifying a reversal is important, and have identified various "types" of reversals and a variety of tapping exercises to resolve each type.

The development of the EFT process kept the concept of resolving reversals and worked to resolve them by using the Setup. As Gary gained more experience, he believed that the issue of "reversals" is more one of "secondary gains," an often unconscious resistance to resolving the problem. He began to see that a "reversal" is simply one more issue to solve with EFT.

We often have some conflict with resolving our issue, some pro and con challenge that needs to be addressed. The Setup—part problem, part acceptance of self *with* that problem—does appear to help address that conflict.

On the pro side, the Setup can be a real "gift" to the user. When we are upset, rarely if ever, do we have positive, accepting self-talk. A Setup begins the process of linking awareness and acceptance and shifting of perception. The concept of pairing a problem with a positive statement about yourself, e.g., I have this problem, *and* I'm still OK, is a novel idea to many people. After all, we are much better at beating ourselves up than creating positive thoughts about ourselves.

On the con side of using a Setup, the statement, "I deeply and completely accept myself," can be too much for some clients to say. Ask if the default statement sounds true to them *right now*. I remember one client who broke into tears hearing the words, and others became emotional and were not able to speak the words. Practitioners who tell the client to "just say it" and begin tapping are missing an opportunity to expand the client's sense of control in his or her life.

We use the client's words in defining the issue, and as reminder phrases, as they tap. Why then do we give them *our* words as the positive statement in the Setup? Don't let your client miss the experience of finding their own statement. What do *they* see about themselves they consider positive?

The benefits of a self-formed statement are many: helps increase rapport, "sneaks up" on the problem, it's respectful, the client can begin to recognize and own a positive within themselves which takes a step toward increased self-worth and empowerment when they often feel they have little of either. [See article on Individualizing Affirmations.]

Despite the benefits of a Setup, the reality is that focusing on a body sensation and tapping without words is *easier* particularly when using EFT on our own.

> **Better to focus and tap with no words than not tap.**

In my 1½-hour Introduction Classes, I've learned that less is more—particularly to total newbies. Tapping on your face and body to feel better does seem a bit bizarre.

We keep it simple. We focus on body sensations and the tapping points. We use a constricted breathing exercise. We pick how our body feels about a current annoyance. If time, we address how to deal with cravings; focusing on the body sensation as they think about their food "weakness." The only Setups used are some version of, "Even though I have [this sensation] in my body, I'm OK." Then, as they focus on their body sensation, we tap.

I mention using EFT for phobias, but generally, we are unable to demonstrate using EFT for a phobia. It is not possible to cover everything in an hour and a half. We discuss using EFT for any upset, no matter the cause. We want to prevent the question, "How do I tap for...?"

I explain and demonstrate over and over the generic instructions for tapping: whatever is going on, focus on the feeling in your body and tap.

Vernon, like some students, thought EFT was "interesting" but did not use it after class. He did not mention in class that he hated going to the dentist, even to have his teeth cleaned.

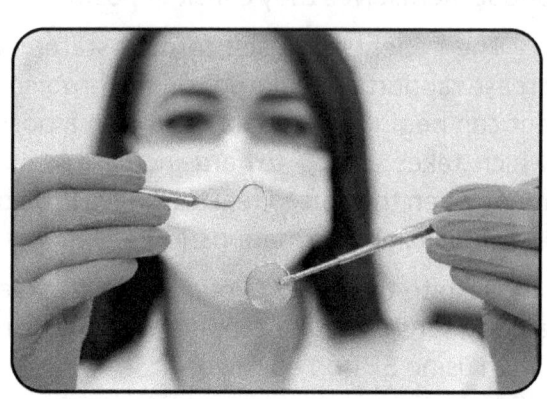

Two months later, time to have his teeth cleaned; Vernon decided to give EFT a try. Later he told me, "I didn't remember all you said, and I forgot some of the points. I just focused on my anxious feeling and tapped a few times, and I wasn't anxious anymore."

It's a common story. And, I saw him again a few months later. He told me he had been calm even through the follow-up visits. He seemed surprised. Wow! I said, encouragingly. But meant it, I am still amazed at the impact just tapping on places on our body has.

Don't get me wrong here, I am not proposing a universal practice of skipping useful parts of EFT, either the Setup or words, certainly not as a practitioner. However, there are times, especially when tapping by yourself, that simply focusing on body sensations and tapping is useful to calm yourself quickly. Even imagining tapping can be powerful.

For a quick result with minimal effort, it is hard to beat simply focusing on the body sensation and tapping. After all, tapping without words is superior to not tapping at all!

NOTES

Credit:

Photo by Yusuf Belek on Unsplash.com

24

Too Much Too Soon

> **IN A NUTSHELL:** Our clients can be outwardly cooperative and appear to engage fully with the practitioner—they can appear ready, willing, and able; everyone's ideal client. You think you had a successful session and in some ways it was. But your client doesn't come back. Your work together may have threatened their identity of self. It was *too much, too soon*. EFT is a powerful tool. It can shift an issue very quickly. However, *just because we can does not mean we should.*

Let's use a hypothetical situation. Sharon re-schedules her first appointment first because her mother needed to go to the store, then again because her daughter needed help paying her insurance. Finally, Sharon comes in for the appointment. In the first few minutes, she makes comments about being depressed and overwhelmed. "My family and friends have so many problems." She says she has trouble sleeping and is exhausted all the time. She doesn't believe that anything can help *her*. She's here because a friend was pushing her to try EFT. She mentions how important it is to her to do what she can to help others. She describes herself as the peacemaker, the go-to person in her circle that everyone can rely on.

> Because we can doesn't mean we should!

Lots of issues here. Lots of "roads" we could explore. Like many clients, Sharon is presenting a multi-faceted problem full of complexity and twists and turns. Sharon is displaying common limiting beliefs:

- If I put my needs/wants/wishes first, I'm selfish.
- I *must* help others; their needs and problems are more important than mine.
- Doing for others is how I hide; if they knew what I was really like they would not like me.
- My value, my worth is in what I can do for others; I feel guilty if I say no.
- I can't complain or say no; I'll be criticized.
- *I* certainly can't get angry; good people don't get angry; when I am angry it proves how awful I really am.

Not surprisingly, Sharon's beliefs spring from formative experiences in her childhood. Parents who were too busy dealing with their own needs (mental illness and alcoholism) to identify and help their child form a positive self-image to believe that she was, and is, important. Sharon, like many such children, took on the role and the identity of caregiver for her parents and siblings. Her needs were discounted. She became convinced that she only had worth through helping others. Her definition of self revolves around being responsible for others at the expense of her own wellbeing.

The practitioner worked to find a specific event. She asked about experiences that Sharon thinks may have led to her current feelings. They decide on which event to begin, and they tap. The session was very focused on tapping.

The fear of rejection, criticism, and the need to be liked at any cost may show up in a session as an *outward* sense of cooperation but with the *inward* fear of losing control. A part of Sharon that serves to protect, a part of her that sees changing her approach to life as dangerous. The "I have to please everyone" part of her leads her to follow the practitioner, the protective part of her is terrified of what will happen.

Sharon is good at hiding her fears—after all, *her* problems/feelings are not important. She's been trained from childhood to meet other's needs, and, even in the session, she works to please. She taps away with the practitioner. They work successfully to resolve a couple of childhood events. As Sharon leaves, she thanks the practitioner for resolving the childhood scenes. Perhaps even a compliment. The practitioner is feeling pretty good!

The problem? Reframing a couple of childhood scenes does not shift a lifetime of beliefs, experiences and habituated behavior. Sharon has had her sense of self threatened. Her protective part is not happy, in fact, terrified. She's done *too much, too soon*. It was too fast; the session threatened her identity and awakened multiple fears. She doesn't return.

> **EFT can be simple; people can be very complex.***

EFT can move too quickly for the readiness of the client with many layers of complex issues. It can threaten protective "parts" of us. We can only move as fast as our most "reluctant" part is willing. Those reluctant parts need to be identified and addressed.

> **Sometimes the fastest way to get there is to slow down.***

Resistance is normal. *We are all reluctant and threatened by change.* We all have our protective parts. Often, we don't recognize what our resistance is. We don't realize what is blocking us from what we consciously say we want to change.

Our resistance, reluctance, hesitancy, fears of change could be reframed as a positive behavior. Those beliefs and/or behaviors we *say* we want to change are the same beliefs and behaviors that have served a very positive purpose somewhere in our life. Our resistance insists that we look at changing very carefully and not rush into other behaviors that we once perceived as "dangerous."

Practitioners help the client identify and *respect* reluctance.

We can help significantly reduce potential resistance by asking non-threatening questions and addressing the fears of changing before attempting to change. Notice I did not say *prevent* resistance. I don't think that is possible; resistance is normal. Recognize and appreciate the role the resistant "part" has played in our life.

Help the client explore their resistance with questions such as:

- ▶ As you think about making changes in your life, what comes up for you?
- ▶ How will changing this behavior impact you?
- ▶ How will this impact *others* in your life?
- ▶ What do you think the response of others would be?
- ▶ What might happen if you got over this?
- ▶ Is there any part of you that might *not* want to change this?
- ▶ What is your theory as to why you do (or think) this?
- ▶ We always have a conflict to change. What do you think your conflict would be?
- ▶ What one thing could we work on today that you believe may help you feel better?

In Sharon's life, her entire support system is created around her sacrifices to others: her husband and children, family, neighbors, friends, and her community. It is logical for her to fear a "change" that would literally modify, perhaps in a significant way, important things in her life.

> **Change is Good. You go first!!**

How many of us are keen to "fix" a problem that will change our life significantly, right away? Change, even good change, can be very scary. Indeed, the change you say you want probably would have happened before now if there were not parts of you holding it in place!

Major lifestyle changes involving shifts in our identity of self often can be—and perhaps really should be—slow going. Digging down to the limiting beliefs and addressing varying resistance takes careful detective work, time, empathy, and lots of listening and patience.

Even after reframing our issues and our beliefs of ourselves, changing the behaviors of many years also takes awareness and real effort. Give lots of enthusiastic reinforcement for even tiny shifts and changes. Never underestimate the power of baby steps. Folks like Sharon, indeed all of us, are truly doing the best we can!

NOTES

*An Annism

25

Pros and Cons of Intakes

IN A NUTSHELL: When we first have contact with a client, there are many questions we *could* ask. Among practitioners, there are probably as many intake formats as there are practitioners. What *is* the best thing to do?

Some practitioners give in-depth questionnaires in advance for a client to complete. Other practitioners don't ask any questions initially and prefer a more open-ended approach, without a list of established questions. Most are somewhere in between. I have experimented with many options. I've changed my intake process many times—don't like any of them! There are many ways to assess one's "ready-willing-ableness."

As I've mentioned many times, people are complex. Some clients don't like sharing a lot of information immediately—they want to "dip their toe in." Or they may not see the intake questions as relevant to their issue—and resent it. Others complete it so superficially or so exaggerated as to be almost meaningless. *How* someone answers a question can be as, or more, important as what they say. All responses give some idea of the client's view of self and the world, of course, but what is the most helpful?

What about making the form optional? What about sharing the information but let them know that this is what we *might* cover; we *may* address together.

Some practitioners like Liz Hart, an experienced master trainer practitioner in New Zealand, give the below handout to new clients to help explain how she works. While the list may be seen as invasive by some, it is an excellent summary of the main factors frequently an issue for many clients. In reviewing this list, the client could begin the process of exploring and perhaps begin the process of viewing their issue from a different perspective. Filling out the form is not required.

Issues We *May* Investigate Together

During our time together we *may be considering* these questions with gentle curiosity. You don't need to know the answers before we begin—we will discover them together. Not all the questions will be relevant to you or your situation. This is just a map of the territory we might cover to help you understand the process.

Identify the Problem

▶ How are you experiencing this problem now?

▶ Can you be specific—Where? What? How? When? Who?

Identify the Feeling

▶ How does having this problem make you feel?

▶ Where do you feel that feeling in your body?

Identify how you feel about other people or things because of this problem.

▶ What does this problem mean about X? X means a relevant person, thing, situation, etc.

▶ How would your perspective of X change if this was not a problem for you?

▶ How does this problem affect your relationship with X?

PROS AND CONS OF INTAKES

- ▶ What would your relationship to X look like if you got over this problem?

Identify core events around:

- ▶ How do you know you have this problem?
- ▶ What is your theory as to why you have this problem?
- ▶ Where did you learn this?
- ▶ What does this feeling remind you of?
- ▶ Where/when else have you felt this way?
- ▶ When did you first feel this way? What about?
- ▶ Who else do you know who has had this problem?

Identify how you feel about yourself:

- ▶ What does having this problem mean *about* you?
- ▶ How do you feel about yourself for having this problem?

Identify any labels others give you for having this problem:

- ▶ How have other professionals described your problem?
- ▶ What do others think/say about you for having this problem?
- ▶ How do they treat you or behave towards you?
- ▶ How do you react to their ideas? Do you believe them?

Identify the "dark side" for wanting to keep this problem:

- ▶ What could be a reason you might want to keep this problem?
- ▶ What would you have to give up if you got over this problem?
- ▶ What would you have to do, or be, different if you got over this problem?

- What is the "saboteur" role in your life? How is your relationship with your "saboteur(s)"?

Identify a way of being you would prefer:

- How would you like to respond to this situation?
- What would be the best possible outcome that could come from this situation?
- Is there a downside to that?
- Would that create another kind of problem for you?

Most people don't know the answers to all these questions when we start working together, and that's okay. EFT helps us feel calmer and more able to consider the questions in helpful ways, so you can resolve what's bothering you and find the best outcome for you. We will begin with some simple questions and gently explore the issues in a way that works for you. If you think of other questions that you are curious about, we can explore those too.

NOTES

Credits:

Thanks to Liz Hart

Photo from her website https://lizhart.com

26

Being vs. Doing

> **IN A NUTSHELL:** Sometimes, we let our *need to do something interfere with actually doing something*. We may need reminding that being fully present and accepting of the person *is doing something* even if it doesn't seem to appear that way.

Sally, an adolescent, was in my office in the treatment program; we were just hanging out, as the kids said. She was sketching on a pad. I started to get a bit antsy that maybe I was wasting our limited time together. I felt we needed to discuss and move toward her goals. She was getting close to discharge. We had worked with EFT several times. I gently asked if there were any issues she'd like to resolve or goals she was having a problem meeting.

Out of the Mouths of Babes

Sally looked up from her sketching and gave me a pained look as only adolescents can, "Miss Ann," she said, "Everybody is always trying to *fix* me. Being with you is the only place

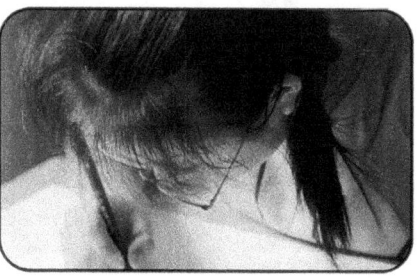

I feel comfortable to *just be me*. Do we need to fix that too?" Gulp. "You're right Sally," I said. "Learning to just *be* is a very important thing."

The ability to be in the moment is an important skill to have! Being in the moment *with* someone significant is a precious gift— to both of you, whatever you are doing.

> **Not all sessions need to be about *doing* therapy or *doing* EFT or *doing* anything.**

Sometimes a client just needs to talk. They need to feel accepted, need to feel understood. When someone is fully present with you, you feel better about you. *Helping someone feel better about themselves while in our presence is a big gift*, if not *the* biggest gift, we share with others. When you are fully present there is no judgment—*judgment needs the past to operate.*

Sometimes being present and accepting is a lot harder than providing an intervention. Years ago, pre-EFT, I taught crisis intervention and active listening skills to volunteers on the crisis hotline for our mental health center. The hardest concept for the volunteers to grasp was learning not to rush to intervene or give suggestions—they wanted to *do something*.

Over and over, I reinforced that the gift of our time, of being there, of listening and accepting, was the greatest action we could take – *it was doing something—something important.*

Utilizing EFT does not change the need to be fully present, to actively listen, to work toward understanding and acceptance. Our desire to *do something* is *our* agenda. The job, the *doing*, is to help the client feel emotionally safe and ready.

> **Listening, working to understand, is doing something.**

No, we don't want our clients to talk on and on, and yes, we do want to help structure the session. Of course, you are going to share your insights and perhaps make a suggestion or offer a resource. We do, however, sometimes forget that helping someone is more than having our client list their issues, tap through their list, find the exact Setup or phrase, and address all the aspects, although those are good things to do. Being present is about providing a safe place to be who they are and respecting that *at this moment in time they are doing the best they can.*

EFT is an efficient tool; progress can be even fast—*after* they feel that you are fully present. That you care enough to work to understand their "frame," that you respect them as they are. That you believe they have the inner resources to resolve their issues, *and* that they feel they are in a safe place to both discover who they are and to practice just *being*.

NOTES

Credit:

Photo by Peng Li on Unsplash

27

In Defense of Resistance

> IN A NUTSHELL: We can *all* be resistant from time to time. Resistance to some degree and ambivalence to change is common, perhaps universal. We don't really, really, want to change. We had rather the situation, or other person change, or even better, our problem to just go away. Change is a lot of work and can be rather scary stuff. Often, there is a conflict. Part of us wants "this" and part of us wants "that." The more resistant, the more fearful of change we are, the more we need empathy—and less questions and slower approaches. The more we should focus on "baby steps."

Resistance is understandable, even necessary. If we didn't resist change, we'd accept every new idea that came along, buy every product, be victims to crooks, not have a sense of being right or a sense of self, not have stability or predictability, and there would be no fighting against injustice (Mitchell, 2012, p.14).

Resistance serves to protect us in some way. Our job as practitioner is to find the "useful purpose" it serves – and to uncover the specific person/place/time, and the when, what, where, and how it was created. We are patient. We modify and adjust to what is in front of us. Experienced practitioners realize that we don't "push the river." Handling client resistance in a session can be challenging. Getting really good at EFT, or any other technique, is not our biggest challenge. The challenge is in gaining rapport, in assessing and calibrating the client, when to ask questions and when not to ask any questions, when not to use your technique, whether to modify and adjust or continue doing what you were doing.

One of the things I love about EFT, and yet perhaps the one most loaded with responsibility for the practitioner, is that EFT can often bypass guardedness or resistance – at least temporarily. We can go faster than the client is ready, we can do "too much, too soon." Ever had what you thought was a successful session in which you both agree that much was accomplished only to have the client be a no show for the next visit they'd agree on? Clients often vote with their feet.

> **Sometimes the fastest way to get there is to slow down.**

Our resistant part(s) believes it performs an important role in keeping us safe—in protecting us from an even worst outcome. Our resistant parts, like our non-resistant parts, need to be heard and listened to and accepted, not to mention appreciated. One approach is to address that part directly. Sometimes a client can go "inside" and listen to what a particular "part" of them has to say. "If you were able to hear what that [resistance] has to say, what do you think it would be saying?" Whatever comes out is relevant; it's all connected and has meaning. If they are unable to "hear" what the part has to say, ask them to use their imagination and "make it up." Other clients are unable or unwilling to try such an exercise.

However we start, we always work to honor and respect whatever the client brings. One way that shows that respect is never to suggest they "just say" the default, "I deeply and completely accept myself," or any derivative thereof. Spend the time to find a positive self-acceptance statement the person believes is true right then.

Richard Swartz, Ph.D., developer of the Internal Family Systems therapy in the 1980s, gives us a list of eight characteristics exhibited when we are in touch with our inner wisdom, our real self: Curiosity, Compassion, Courage, Calm, Connection, Creativity, Confidence, Clarity. These are a beautiful definition of when we are "in the zone" with our clients. Anything other than these characteristics means that you, or your client, remain in a place of resistance or fear.

> Curiosity
> Compassion
> Courage
> Connection
> Creativity
> Confidence
> Clarity

Clarity doesn't mean you know everything. Clarity also means you are comfortable in knowing what you don't know. Clarity means that you are constantly working on increasing your on awareness of your own biases. Confidence doesn't mean you are always 100% sure what to say and do, but you are confident that you will do the best you can, that your goal is for the highest and best outcome for your client.

We often see an increase in these characteristics in ourselves and clients as we use EFT to resolve the issues. These characteristics could be a list of the side effects of EFT! They are certainly very good reasons to continue our own self-awareness journey with EFT.

Resistance indicates a fear of something worse than the current challenge. These fears could be layered. You may be self-sabotaging because you feel inferior in some way, but a deeper reason could be that you are so afraid of the pain of failing that you make sure you sabotage every opportunity. After all you cannot fail if you don't try. If the solution to your problem is terrifying, you are not going to see that solution. Remember: If you don't see you have an option; you don't have an option.***

Resistance as a Mismatch

In *Effective Techniques for Dealing with Highly Resistant Clients*, Clifton Mitchell says resistance is often *a mismatch between what the practitioner is doing and the client is willing to accept*. Mitchell says we are not helpful when we are working harder than our client, are trying to convince the client of something, worry more about their problem than they do, dread the session, or feel drained in an unhealthy way after the session.

Mitchell goes on to say that resistance can occur:

—when the practitioner wants *more* for the client than they want, at least right then, or

—when the practitioner is too intent on their own agenda. This can show up in thoughts or comments such as, "I am trying to get them to...," "if only he would..." "If only I could..." "I wish they...," or

—when trying to solve the problem for the client, or

—when going at a faster pace than the client is comfortable, or

—asking a question at an unacceptable time or way.

How many times have we told a client you cannot change someone else, you can only change yourself? And yet, what do we often work to do? Change the client!

What we can do, *and is impossible not to do*, is to influence our clients. We influence *with everything we say and do, and everything we do not say and do*. We are "constantly adjusting and matching [our] method of influence with client's current state of mind." The problem occurs when our "method of influence is mismatched" to the client's current willingness to accept it (Mitchell, 2012, p. 10). Clients may come to the session with their own resistance. It is our job to give them nothing to resist against.

Dealing with Internal Conflicts

Clients may make a statement similar to, "*Part of me wants this, and another part of me wants that.*" Or, "I'm of two minds about that." Our bodies are not really divided into parts. However, we all have inner conflicts and various, sometimes contradictory, ways we choose to react/behave. There is always a conflict, a pro/con to change. If we weren't conflicted, we would have changed already. As Joni Mitchell famously said, "Something's lost, and something's gained in living everyday." When the client is aware of the conflict, we often address those conflicts directly with Setups like

- "Even though part of me *is not* willing to ___ and I feel ___ in my body when I think about it because I'm afraid it won't change (or that it will change), I accept myself and maybe, perhaps, I can accept that that part of me."

> **We can only move as fast as our most reluctant "part."**

When the Timing is Right

While many of our clients are or can become somewhat "resistant," fortunately most of our clients are *not highly* resistant. Some come to see us highly motivated to change. Such highly motivated clients are easy. We all love those. And when an otherwise motivated client reaches a "stuck" point, often a couple of Setups addressing our natural resistance to change is all it takes for the client to move forward.

We examine the conflicts, tap through whatever experiences created and reinforced the belief, perception, and/or behavior keeping someone stuck. And, we have some great exploratory questions we can use:

▶ How do you feel about having this problem so long?

▶ What is your theory about why this continues to be a problem?

▶ Who in your life might be upset if you were to change?

▶ Or the ready, willing, able type question: What do you think gets in your way?

▶ What comes up when you think about addressing/resolving/changing this?

▶ What have you tried before?

▶ When did the behavior or belief, start? What was happening then? Who was involved?

▶ Or, when is the first time you were aware this was a problem?

▶ How is this protecting us, i.e., what job does it do?

▶ What keeps us hanging on to the mindset or behavior?

▶ What do we need now for that resistant "part" of us to feel safe to change "jobs" or maybe "retire?"

And When the Timing is <u>Not Right</u>?

Whether you call it being "stuck," not yet ready, reluctance or resistance, the best strategy is to slow down. Increase the amount of silence in the session, pause more often. Increase the space between your words. Use less questions, more empathic comments. Use statements such as, *share with me*, or *tell me about* or *I am curious as to...*, instead of direct questions. State what they are doing in an empathic, positive, potential solution-oriented way: "You seem to have difficulty *right now* with *finding the right words* to describe what you mean." Clarify more. Work on very small pieces of an issue. *Focus on baby steps.*

Sometimes the "person/place/time" we search for is in the relationship between you and the client at a particular time. Share what you experience in the moment, "As you talk about this, I notice a great sadness coming up in me and I'm curious if you may be feeling that too." "I notice that when you mention your brother, your body seems to tighten up; I'm wondering what that could mean."

IN DEFENSE OF RESISTANCE

Any movement is positive movement, no matter how small.

Never underestimate the power of baby steps.

NOTES

Credit: Baby step photo by Jukan Takeis on Unsplash.com

Effective Techniques for Dealing with Highly Resistant Clients by Clifton Mitchell, clifton-mitchell.com

***Internal Family Systems* book by Robert Swartz on Amazon.com

***An Annism.

28

Is Reframing Necessary?

> IN A NUTSHELL: Reframing is probably the most misunderstood and most difficult of the EFT concepts. Reframes composed of meaningful and relevant words, offered at the most fertile time in the session and relationship, and delivered in a way that is meaningful to the client, can undoubtedly speed the perceptual change about an issue. But don't rush into reframing. *Reframes are not a critical part of EFT, the actual reframing of an issue is up to the client.* Frequently, clients come up with their own cognitive shift or reframing, for their issue.

When tapping is utilized to effectively clear an issue, when sufficient aspects are neutralized, a new perspective or reframe by the client for that issue often occurs—naturally. The physical *sensations* may change, the scene *looks* different, *sounds* different; *interpreted* differently. *Cognitive shifts that arise from decreasing intensity are the most powerful of reframes.*

Practitioners can feel pressured to create the *right reframe* and, of course, at the *right time* and the *right way* for it to "land" with the client. Reframes that don't land can "derail" a session or temporarily break the rapport you worked to establish, at times permanently.

The role of the practitioner is to help the client find and resolve the many aspects of the events impacting their issue. Granted, working through event after event and detail after detail is time-consuming; it is work. But don't be too quick to offer a reframe.

I remember a story told by a psychiatrist who ran (non-EFT) therapy groups for women who had been molested as children. He would repeat across many group sessions that "you were just a child; it was not your fault." Finally, one member of the group spoke up, "Stop telling me that! I *know* I was just a child!! Telling me that does *not* take away my guilt and shame and anger."

In the chapter about phobias, I pointed out that most reframes we offer, and cognitive shifts clients come to, are not overly brilliant insights. Most are rational, common-sense statements that the client already *intellectually* knows. When they are upset, the cognitive ability to accurately assess the situation is lowered. That's why the recommendation is that, *before* offering a reframe, the client's intensity levels are four or below. That's why client readiness and timing may be critical when delivering an effective reframe. That's why working through the emotions around the event is necessary. That's why checking with the client as to the accuracy of the wording you use while tapping is important.

The best reframes you offer are often intuitive—they come from your inner voice of wisdom. Your intuitive ability—your ability to hear that inner voice—increases when you become aware of and clear enough of your internal chatter to be able to listen to your inner wisdom. Increasing your awareness leads to increased intuition, increased ability to assess the timing, and to recognize the impact of the reframe on the client and adjust accordingly.

An example of a well-timed, relevant—but not brilliant—reframe that landed was with Alexandrea. She had been in a fire as a child and was terrified of a fire starting in her home. This anxiety had increasingly spread to other areas of her life. Over several sessions, as she worked through the complex emotions surrounding the experiences that led to her fears, we began working on her obsessively checking everything in her house over and over before she left the house or before she went to bed. As her anxiety decreased, she realized it was her anxiety that drove the need to triple check to make sure everything was turned off, unplugged, locked, and secured. Her overall intensity had decreased to three on the zero to ten scale.

Toward the end of the session, she said, "My life is controlled by the fear and I hate that." As we tapped around this new insight, I offered, "*I can be cautious without being fearful.*" She stopped tapping, laughed, and said, "Of course! I don't need the anxiety to check for safety in my home." I smiled back and asked how she could use that new understanding in her life before our next session. She thought a bit and said she'd come up with a checklist of things to be checked. She said she'd use the list to check everything *once*. "That way, I will know it is done and not worry about it. If I do start to feel anxious and tempted to go check again, I'll tap." "Great idea," I said.

Sometimes, like in the above story, you immediately know the reframe "landed." In other situations, you may want to clarify, "Does that fit? Is there a better way to put it?" "What happened when I said that?"

When the reframe does not land, a simple admission like, "Well, that didn't work! What is your thought about this?" usually works to maintain rapport. Adding a "waffle" word such as: perhaps, yet, maybe, stated in a questioning tone can help acceptance and lead the brain to assess the possibility. how do you know that? Or, How did you come to that conclusion? What does doing that, having that, problem mean *about* you?

Successful sessions do not always need a reframe. Asking meaningful and thought-provoking questions can also shift perceptions. Have you thought about/considered [that]? How does doing [that] help (or not help) you? In the next chapter we'll look at the "steps" for successful reframes.

NOTES

Resource: More on Reframing from my chapter in *Clinical EFT Handbook Vol 1*, a collection from EFT experts.

29

How to Create Reframes

> **IN A NUTSHELL:** To be effective, a reframe must be offered at the right time, with the right words, delivered in the right way for the client to accept. One of the challenges in learning how-to-do reframes is that few resources give how-to instructions for creating effective reframes. Maya de Vries, EFT Founding Master and personal development coach in Germany, offers nine aspects to be considered in delivering successful reframes.

Our core beliefs frame our lives. We develop these beliefs from our past experiences. Some beliefs are positive, some negative and limit our life and the ability to reach our potential. Reframes, when used at the right time, can be useful in aiding the client to a new perspective and shift a negative belief to a more realistic one.

Since clients often form their own cognitive shift, don't be too quick to use a reframe; it may not be needed. Many reframes are common sense statements such as, "that was then, this is now," that we "know" logically. Reducing the intensity of the issue helps us *know* it on an emotional level as well.

Nine Factors to be Considered When Offering a Reframe.*

Maya de Vries watched Gary Craig conduct sessions on EFT videos over and over. As she watched, she broke down the various "parts" of successful reframes and came up with nine "steps" for reframing.

The first step needs to be first. The last step needs to be last. The in-between steps can be fluid depending on the client. As always, timing is critical. While all the steps should be considered, not all steps are required for every client, every time. The necessity for you to be successful at delivering other EFT techniques and have the ability to carefully calibrate the client's response *before* utilizing reframes still applies.

#1: To enhance client motivation, willingness, and readiness to change. Look for the limiting beliefs. Acknowledge the courage to release the problem and present the possibility of a new perspective, e.g., *"Even though _____, I dare to be willing to release this problem in my life and open a window to see it differently, where I can define my angle of view."* Find the reigning dysfunctional belief and personal truth which resulted from this life experience. Look for the "writing on the walls," the beliefs the client operates under in the world. You need to identify the "frame" through which they see themselves, others, and the world. You are looking for the beliefs that make up an "eleventh commandment" in their world, e.g., I must, I always, I can never.

#2: *Find Client's reigning dysfunctional belief/personal truth* which resulted from this life experience. Ask questions to discover the client's "writings on his walls," the beliefs around how the world works that could be behind the event: *What did that experience convey to you about the world? What did you learn from this experience at the time it happened? How did this experience influence the rest of your life?* You are looking for a client *statement that sounds like an 11th commandment* for them. Listen for words like, all of...are..., or I always..., I can never..., I always must...

#3: Facilitate the client's awareness that there is a conflict between the logical and the emotional mind. Ask questions such as how true is this for you now? Do you think that is always logical? The client may respond that they know it is not logical, but it is "true for me." Beliefs are like the glue that sticks the problems together; dissolve the glue, unstick the realistic cognitive thoughts. One possibility is to use gentle exaggeration and humor. Tap for reasons they may not want to let it go.

#4: To encourage the client and increase their sense of empowerment, reinforce their strengths and abilities. Find power resources in the past. What have they successfully handled in the past? For example, *...I survived this belief, and even if I don't want to let it go, I realize I have already overcome other problems in my life.*

#5: Enhance their understanding and compassion for feelings they had during the situation in the past, and the actions and reactions when it happened. *What happened? What did you do or not do?* Address the details of the experience. Enhance the client's emotional frame from the past and treat the experience from a new perspective. Find that specific event and work gently toward the worse moment. Tap for the feelings the child had – guilt, shame, sadness, hurt. *...I am no longer the person I was then, have more resources now.*

#6: Release self-destructive thought patterns addressing all aspects as untreated aspects will influence the next two steps. Stop client self-judgment, self-blame, anger, and criticism toward the self for whatever role they played, what they did or did not do, in what happened.

#7: Enhance client understanding and compassion for the actions of others involved. This does not mean they need to *approve* of what happened or the other people involved. Be careful with the concept of forgiveness; wait until the client asks, never force. *Forgiveness is not always necessary or the goal.* Work on any residual emotions not released earlier and toward acceptance of what happened and awareness that it is over, and they survived.

#8: Help the client to reach a state of complete acceptance of what happened to the point where they can fully release the negative emotions. Help them to stop feeling victimized, e.g., *...I did* *what I did, I was a child, I did what children do.*

#9: Help the client to transform the "bad" experience into a source of power. Guide them towards reclaiming the energy from this experience to be available to them now. Clients often "sense" an internal change: a body sensation, tingling, cooling, movement, etc. Reframe ideas: *...don't know why it happened, don't need to know why to open up to a deeper truth, and benefit from the wisdom that came from it.*

Reframing is an advanced technique. A mentor can be beneficial in becoming skillful using EFT techniques and reframing skills. There are many ways to share reframes. Gary Craig listed common themes of reframes are:

State the obvious in a unique way:

Even though I'm terrified there will be a fire in the house, I can be cautious instead of fearful.

Identify similarities:

Even though it makes me "crazy" when my boyfriend tries to solve all my problems, he pushes all the same buttons as my father.

Recognize personal responsibility:

Even though my brother said that hateful thing, it is my reaction to his words that hurt.

Address stubborn beliefs:

Even though I still want to blame my mother for my problems, I can let go of "this" event.

Consider forgiveness:

Even though she wrote that nasty email, I realize she has her own problems.

Create humor:

See the comedy in the situation or reduce it to the ridiculous. Even though I react to all rejection as I did in first grade, I'm taking the problem-solving advice of a 6-year-old.

Conservative common sense reframes:

I was doing the best I could. I was just a child. I understand *now* how I did that.

She was trying to protect me. He was a wounded soul. It was my reaction that hurt me.

The accident wasn't my fault. I was just there. Of course, I make mistakes; I'm only human.

That was then; this is now.

Adding qualifiers to help reframes land:

Perhaps, maybe, someday, consider, might, probably, may, think about, could, will, possibly, yet or, I can let go of this tiny percent.

NOTES

More on Reframing from my chapter in *Clinical EFT Handbook Vol 1* - a collection from EFT experts.

*The nine steps are summarized from **Nine Steps of Reframing** by Maya de Vries, in a presentation given at the 2007 EFT International Masterclass. Maya conducted a demonstration that includes many examples of reframes. DVD available from https://annadams.com/product/the-9-steps-of-reframing-with-maya-de-vries/

30

The Beginning of Research into Energy Psychology

> **IN A NUTSHELL:** One of the less well-known names in the energy psychology world is Charles Figley, Ph.D. In 1994, Figley was the Traumatology Institute Director at Florida State University. Dr. Figley had been a Marine in Vietnam and had a personal interest in working to resolve the psychological problems of returning Vietnam veterans. "Combat trauma is more an injury that needs healing than an illness which needs medicine," wrote Figley. In a search for effective treatments for PTSD, Figley sent an invitation around the country to his colleagues for alternative approaches to treating trauma.

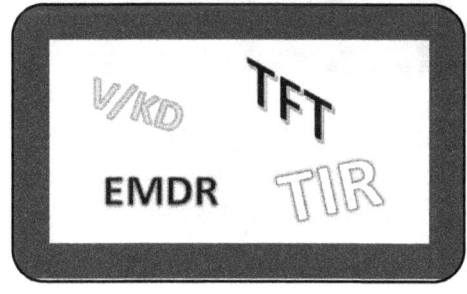

Four methods were chosen for a weeklong trial of the alternative techniques. Selected elected were: Trauma Incident Reduction (TIR), Eye Movement Desensitization and Resolution (EMDR), Visual Kinesthetic Dissociation (V/KD) a NLP technique called Rewind and Thought Field Therapy (TFT).

The study was the first attempt to compare the effectiveness of these relatively new techniques. While the project could not officially be called research, it did call significant attention to TFT. Figley was impressed enough to send a letter to his colleagues in 1995 saying, *...we are [not] suggesting that [TFT] is better than any other approach. All four of the approaches we investigated generated impressive results. But TFT stood out from all other approaches of which I am aware because of five reasons:*

- *It is extraordinarily powerful, in that clients receive nearly immediate relief from their suffering and the treatment appears to be permanent.*

- *It can be taught to nearly anyone so that clients can not only treat themselves but treat others affected.*

- *It appears to do no harm.*

- *It does not require the client to talk about their troubles, something that often causes more emotional pain and discourages many for seeking treatment.*

- *It is extremely efficient (fast and long-lasting).*

With his wife Kathy, who retired at the end of 2014, Figley taught and mentored thousands of helping professionals to increase their knowledge of dealing with trauma. In 1997, Figley was instrumental in establishing the Green Cross Academy of Traumatology. As the website GreenCross.org states, the academy is "to bring together world leaders in the study of traumatology to establish and maintain professionalism and high standards for this new field."

Green Cross is "an international, humanitarian assistance organization, non-profit corporation comprised of trained traumatologists and compassion fatigue service providers. Most are licensed mental health professionals; all focused on helping people in crisis following traumatic events."

Figley is a true pioneer in trauma and particularly in what is now known as PTSD. His first book, *Stress Disorders among Vietnam Veterans: Theory, Research, and Treatment,* was published in 1978. It was the first to discuss what later was named post-traumatic stress disorder. He has since written several books about treating trauma. As of 2020, Charles Figley is at Tulane University.

Figley's letter is published on several websites. He later wanted to withdraw the letter and his endorsement as the field of energy psychology was not accepted by other mental health professional bodies.

> Volume 59 NO. 9 September 2003
>
> Journal of
> ## Clinical Psychology
>
> Evaluation of a Meridian-Based Intervention, Emotional Freedom Techniques (EFT), for Reducing Specific Phobias of Small Animals
>
> 30 minutes of EFT vs. deep breathing
>
> **Wells, S., Polglase, K., Andrews, H.B., Carrington, P., & Baker, A.H.**
> Curtin University of Technology of Western Australia
>
> *An exciting breakthrough in a peer reviewed journal*

In 2003 the first official research using EFT was published in a peer-review journal, Journal of Clinical Psychology. Currently, there are hundreds of studies and research listed on the Association for Comprehensive Energy Psychology (ACEP) energypsych.org site.

Trivia: ACEP was created in 1999. Fred Gallo had the energypsych.com name site *before* ACEP created energypsych.org; the organization would have liked the .com site as well. Fred Gallo was the first to coin the term Energy Psychology. He has written several books—all are recommended for the serious student. His website states that he owns the Registered Trademark ® for the term Energy Psychology.

NOTES

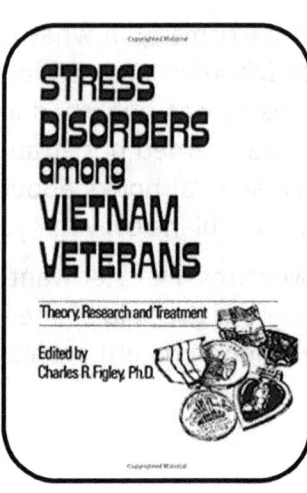

Useful Resources for more information: https://energypsych.org

https://www.thetraumatherapistproject.com/

https://greencross.org/

Read about Figley's many accomplishments in the trauma field: https://charlesfigley.com/biography

Figley's book: *Stress Disorders among Vietnam Veterans: Theory, Research, and Treatment* available from amazon.com

Credit:

Figley photo from Tulane University

Journal slide from EFT4PowerPoint V3020 EFT Workshop in a Box. https://www.EFT4powerpoint.com

31

How Gary Craig Got into the VA

> **IN A NUTSHELL:** Gary Craig, not a mental health professional, released the **Six Days at the VA** videos in the late '90s, we EFTers all wondered, how did he do that? Getting EFT into *the* VA has not been an easy task; there is no "the" VA as VA hospital directors around the country all have a bit different approach. The question was answered in a presentation at the 2000 ACEP (Association for Comprehensive Energy Psychology) Conference by Floyd Meshad – "call me Shad."

Shad Meshad served one tour as a Social Work/Psychology Officer in South Vietnam. He described his job in Vietnam as giving peace of mind in an impossible place. Upon his return, he was asked to help set up programs for the Brentwood  Veterans Affairs hospital in California. He was a logical choice, Shad was a veteran, a trained mental health professional, already with experience treating soldiers. He ran the Vietnam Veterans Re-Socialization Unit for eight years working with Vietnam veterans with severe readjustment problems in the Los Angeles area.

Shad attended Gary's three-hour training in San Francisco with about 80 mental health professionals. Shad was skeptical—weren't we all—but tried using EFT at dinner on various issues with a friend and was impressed with the results.

Gary called three days later, following up on class attendees, asking what Shad thought of EFT; he replied, "Interesting." Gary gained an invitation to work with volunteers from a veterans group Shad ran for chronic alcohol and drug issues. Gary spent several days in the VA facility filming his sessions with the veterans, which became Craig's *6 Days at the VA* videos. While those videos are no longer available for purchase, there is at least one of the sessions on YouTube.

NOTE: Gary told me later that no other staff from the VA came in to see what was going on. From all indications, this was a one-shot "under the radar" performance. VA's around the country are not "cookie-cutter" operations, and procedures vary from VA to VA.

Shad knew Charles Figley, Ph.D., who organized the first study that compared tapping with other innovations. He was instrumental in getting energy work into the Figley research project. When Figley was proposing comparing alternative methods for effectiveness, Shad told him about EFT and TFT. Figley wanted a mental health professional in the study. He chose TFT as Roger Callahan Ph.D., the developer of TFT, was a licensed psychologist in California.

Shad and Figley both participated in massive anti-war protests by Vietnam Veterans against the war. They both, often together, presented all over the world to increase public awareness and study of Post-Traumatic Stress Disorder or PTSD.

TRIVIA - More about Shad

Shad Meshad was the Founder of the National Veterans Foundation and has led the organization for more than 40 years. He received his master's degree in psychiatric social work from Florida State University and enlisted in the army in 1970, where he served as a counselor for U.S. soldiers in Vietnam. He founded and directed the Vietnam Veterans Re-Socialization Unit at the VA Hospital in Los Angeles, California.

Shad lobbied President Jimmy Carter for the National Vietnam Veterans Readjustment Bill to create the Vet Center Outreach Program, which now serves veterans in more than 300 locations across America. He received many awards for his work and contributions. He serves on the faculty of the International Critical Incident Foundation and many other worthy foundations. He helped first responders during the 9/11 tragedy by training the critical incident and trauma teams at Ground Zero.

Today, in addition to heading the NVF, Shad consults and offers trauma-informed training to mental health, law enforcement, and critical incident professionals.

NOTES

Credits:

Photo from https://www.americamagazine.org/issue/754/article/soldiers-homecoming

Info on Shad Meshad from https://www.linkedintoveterans.com/speakers-experts/ downloaded 7/31/2020.

32

It Worked!! It Worked!! It Worked!!

> **IN A NUTSHELL:** Tim, a counselor in private practice, sent the below email about his experience using EFT with a client the day after completing one of my EFT Level 2 classes. Enjoy sharing in his enthusiasm and the success of his story, used with permission. His email subject line was: *It Worked!! It Worked!! It Worked!!*

As always, I've edited the story to remove any identifying information about the client. Notice how Tim starts by using EFT with the breath, often a good place to start, and then simply tells the client, let's add in some words. Note, too, his surprise when the process worked. Even after 20 years of EFT, I still share his "wow" feeling.

Dear Ann, First off, I really enjoyed the training this weekend, and I wanted to tell you my first EFT story. In two words—it worked! I saw a client tonight whom I've seen for over 5 years. One of those people who are extremely anxious and meets the world with fear. She came in with a very upsetting incident that happened over the weekend and described it as non-traumatic, but very intense. She had put her friend and herself in a very dangerous situation.

This is not a very talkative client, but after sharing the story, something inside me said "it's okay to tap on this." So, I did!!! I kinda surprised myself that I was that open to doing it.

I explained the basic process of what EFT and tapping was. (I found I need some practice doing this). I stumbled through it, but I believe I got my point across. I explained it first as a relaxation technique and did the constricted breathing exercise. Her breathing went from 50% to 75%!

I then said that we were **going to add in some words**. I saw EFT work right in front of my eyes. After three tapping sequences, the anxiety level went from an 8 to a 4, and then to a 2. We ran out of time, it takes longer than you think, and I didn't want to tap anymore to give us some time to process.

The client reported, "I'm so much less anxious than when I came in. I feel that I have the ability to face my week and all things I need to do to repair what I've done."

My therapist face and voice said, "I'm so glad." My internal voice said, "You've got to be freaking kidding me!" We went over the tapping points again, and I wrote down a few setup statements and asked her to use them with tapping a few times a day, and we rescheduled for next week.

Ann, I've experienced this firsthand with a client. It really does work!

Let's stay in touch.

Take good care,

--Tim

33

Pendulums and Jugs

> **IN A NUTSHELL:** Using a pendulum to assess the client's subconscious creates another layer of complexity, another potential step further from the client. It is no longer a joint effort between practitioner and client. Granted, we may all be "connected," but we are assuming a lot here! On the other hand, while self-muscle testing still has challenges and complexities that require a lot of practice in "getting out of your own way," it removes the possibility of influence from another.

Some practitioners use a pendulum exclusively when working with clients. One practitioner went so far as to test which of several different pendulums to use; then used the chosen pendulum to decide which energy technique to utilize from her long list of options.

Muscle testing of any kind is *not useful* for the big questions of life, such as, should I move, should I look for a different job, is my husband having an affair, is my best friend mad at me. These do *not* easily fall into the categories of who, what, when, where. The best results are from specific questions that ask for specific answers. Muscle testing is not a view of the future.

Self-Muscle Test with a Pendulum – Even given the above, pendulums and other self-muscle testing techniques can, at times, be useful. And I'll have to admit, certainly entertaining. Probably the easiest method to access our inner self—or whatever we get in touch with—is by using a pendulum. Don't need anything fancy; a piece of thread around a light ring will work. Hold the thread between thumb and forefinger, straight down without moving the fingers. It may take a while, especially at first, to elicit a response to your request.

I first learned about pendulums in 1974 from a book on self-hypnosis. I tied a ring to a string and followed instructions. I asked for a yes response, then a response for no, then I don't know, and I don't want to answer. The pendulum responded! Surprised and somewhat freaked, I loudly said, "STOP." And, it stopped—immediately! That was too much. I dropped it on the floor like a hot potato. I had no background that would fit or explain this experience.

You may need to gently swing it in a circle slowly to get it moving. Ask the question and it answers your request—usually within seconds. If there is no response or an unclear response, reword the question more specifically to elicit a specific response.

All muscle testing can give a yes or no response. A helpful option when using a pendulum, not available in other muscle testing methods, is the ability to ask for an "I don't know," and "I don't want to answer" response. The last two questions allow more flexibility of feedback and help cover those gray areas (those with less than a 100% answer) or let you know your question wasn't narrow enough. It can take a few tries to find a clear answer. *Using a pendulum does take a bit of practice.*

The pendulum responses for yes and no are not always the same from person to person. Indeed, it may change for yourself over time. Check every time you pick up the pendulum. Clarity of the question, and not expecting a particular answer, are important factors in any muscle testing or pendulum practice, i.e., *do not be attached to the outcome.*

Other Options – There are many ways to test for responses. Two of the most popular are:

Use Just Your Fingers – Make your ring finger and your thumb of one hand into a tight circle. Using the middle finger of your other hand attempt to break the circle. Check how a "tight hold" feels. Then say, YES, hesitate a split second, then attempt to pull the finger circle apart. The fingers should stay tight. Then say NO and pull. You should feel the fingers either come apart or perhaps only a slight "give" where the fingers join.

The Gallon Jug – Take an empty gallon jug and fill it with just enough water that you can comfortably hold up with one outstretched arm. Say YES and note what happens. Say NO, and somehow the jug seems heavier and may drop down a bit. If nothing happens, you may try adding more water and try again.

Create Specific Questions

Detailed focused questions are critical for meaningful answers. Spiraling down with your questions often leads to remembering a specific event you can resolve with tapping. Start with one of the following categories and narrow down to discover the specific who, what, when, where. The category where you begin doesn't matter.

WHO: Does my response to this issue relate to a thing? A person? A man? A woman? Is this woman a community leader? A school employee? A relative? My aunt? My mother?

WHERE: Did this happen in the community? School? Church? At home? Was it in the kitchen? Bedroom? Dining room?

WHEN: How old was I? 0 to 5? 5 to 10? 10 to 15? When you get a yes, narrow it down one year at the time. Was I 15? 14? 13? Was it at supper? At bedtime?

WHAT: Was it something my mother said at the table? Was it my mother's response to something I said? My father? What I did? What I didn't do? What my father did, didn't do? Was there a specific part of what he did that impacts this? Is it his facial expression? His hands, other movements? Was anyone else involved in this? What percentage of [this] is still active? One suggestion to test for a percentage is to draw a circle and mark off 10, 20, 30, 40 … 100.

EFT IS SIMPLE—PEOPLE ARE COMPLEX

And last reminder: Don't make important life decisions based on muscle testing—whether you are doing the testing or someone else is doing it for you. There are indeed things that can go wrong, and situations are often not clear cut. Even though you may work at asking narrow and clear yes or no questions, life is not always yes or no, black or white.

NOTES

Credit: Pendulum photo by author.

34

The Problem vs. *My* Problem

> **IN A NUTSHELL:** Part of our goal in working with others is to help our clients see the difference between, I *am* [this emotion], as compared to [this emotion] is what I am feeling *now*.

Ongoing mentoring or supervision is important for all practitioners—no matter how experienced. We all need support, need to bounce ideas and various opinions around, need to question our perspectives, receive meaningful feedback, and to be challenged. We need help to explore blind spots and increase awareness.

Once I shared a video with my mentor, used with permission for that purpose, dealing with significant and complex grief. In reviewing the video, the psychologist who was not an EFT practitioner, asked why I used the term *"the grief."* A common therapeutic philosophy is having the client acknowledge the emotion as "my grief" to recognize, own the emotion, begin the process of accepting it, and develop strategies for dealing with *his* emotion.

"I see it differently," I replied. "I was encouraging the client to see *'the grief'* that's going on now as only one part of who he is. Grief is an emotion; it is what we feel in the moment. Grief does not define who we are. It is the difference between saying, "I am grief," versus, "grief is what I feel right now; it is not who I am."

The language we use can be powerful. The wording of our questions, summaries, and comments, all impact the session and client and help them reframe their view of self and the world.

As a therapist and supervisor, I often learned from my clients and students. The above approach came from my experience with a couple of clients from my social worker days: "Jeanne" had cancer, and "Minerva" suffered from diabetes. They were similar in many ways: age, economic group, education, race, religion, marital status, even number of children. Their presenting problems were similar. The difference in their approach to their problems was striking. More so since they were scheduled to see me on the same day. Jeanne referred to "cancer" as a problem to be addressed. Minerva, with rather severe diabetes, referred to her disease as "my diabetes" and gave it as a reason/excuse for everything she did or didn't do.

Once I got into the EFT energy world, I quickly understood that whatever the emotion, it is only energy—an energy imbalance that can be neutralized. *Emotion is merely the name our body gives to our physical manifestation of the emotion.*

We benefit from increasing awareness of what we are feeling and from taking responsibility for it. But grief or anger or frustration or overwhelm, etc., are feelings, simply energy. The emotion is *not who we are.*

NOTES

Credit: Photo by whoislimos from unsplash.com

35

Are You as Good as You Could Be?

> **IN A NUTSHELL:** Jeff Goins, author of *How to Become Better Than You Ever Thought Possible*, states, "Why are some people so good at what they do whereas others struggle with the most basic of tasks? Ever wondered if you were capable of achieving more in your work and life?"

Goins shares a story about Mozart, who most believe was an unusually gifted musician. Mozart's father was a musician. He worked with Mozart almost full time from the age of 4. Goins states that Mozart, by age 7, had put in as many hours of practice as a graduate from the Juilliard School in New York City. Goins says that Mozart had the same gift *"we all are born with...the ability to learn, and grow, and adapt."* In addition, Mozart was taught during the critical period when our brains learn the fastest.

Goins went on to say, *"people who appeared to be 'gifted,' were in fact, no more gifted than you or I. They had just learned how to practice."*

Let that sink in and register. They *learned* how to practice. Learning how-to practice was *not* in my school curriculum. I was told "to" practice but was not taught "how." *Focused practice*—what Goins calls "deliberate practice"—is unusual.

Many people never learn this skill. Years ago, one of my mentors, in a field other than mental health, told me not to worry about competition from those who said they have been in the field for 20 years. Many of those, he said, simply have one year of practice repeated 20 times! The concept of effective, *focused practice*—deliberate practice—is, apparently, *not* a common practice!

> **Expertise is never an accident.**

Deliberate practice is learning how to *practice in a focused way*, to practice specific behaviors, and receive feedback from others with more experience than you. Too many people see feedback as criticism. By shying away from the opportunity for meaningful feedback they miss a huge opportunity to grow. Receiving truthful feedback is a gift. Effective practitioners find people who will respectfully give honest feedback. It is our insecurity, our fears of inadequacy, that interprets respectful honest feedback as criticism. To practice for your own increased expertise, mentors are invaluable in helping you identify areas for your focused practice.

Malcolm Gladwell popularized the concept of 10,000 hours to mastery. But it is *not just hours.* You can practice the same hour 10,000 times and still not improve. It is knowing *what* to focus upon as you practice. Having feedback with a mentor for your needed areas of concentration means you benefit from someone else's experience, maybe even their "10,000 hours."

Goins continues with three suggestions to excellence. [*Goin's quotes are bold and in italics.*]

First: ***"What you think about, you become."***

Henry Ford is given credit for saying, "If you think you can or you think you can't, you're right."

Second: *If you're not achieving greatness, then it may be time to* ***surround yourself with others who will challenge you to grow."***

Surround yourself with others who share your goals, with mentors dedicated to increasing your awareness and knowledge, with mentors who give meaningful feedback as to areas for improvement. Such mentors are invaluable.

Goin then states, "*We all love heroic tales of overnight success, but the truth is that expertise is never an accident. Without the right training, peak performance is practically impossible.*"

Deliberate practice means you "*push yourself past what you think is possible.*" And, while I'm quoting let's use a couple more. Susan Jeffers: "Feel the Fear and Do It Anyway." Nike: "Just Do It." These are great statements, all certainly easier said than done.

We do our self-work to deal with our emotional brain full of negative and limiting beliefs and emotions. We can make great progress "doing our own work," but working with an experienced person increases results, decreases time, and builds knowledge and awareness.

Third: Goins says in addition to mindset and deliberate practice, it is important to **"Get around greatness."** It's not just a mindset or practice that affects our performance. It's also our environment. This means that **putting yourself around others who will challenge you** and help you grow is *essential* to mastering any skill.

> **Surround yourself with others who will challenge you to grow.**

The moral of this story is to surround yourself with people who are very good at doing what you want to become very good at doing. People who will give you well-thought-out, honest, meaningful feedback and areas for focused practice are invaluable to becoming the best you can be. Find a group of others working toward excellence, and a mentor, who will help your "protector parts" feel safe enough to go deeper.

NOTES

Credit: The statements in italics can be found: http://michaelhyatt.com/

36

EFT and NLP

> **IN A NUTSHELL:** Gary Craig studied Neuro-Linguistic Programming (NLP) before he learned about utilizing acupuncture points for resolving emotional issues. The NLP presuppositions blend well with EFT, and EFT reflects Gary's knowledge of NLP.

We each have individual presuppositions or beliefs that guide our life—what we consider most important, what we focus on, what we think, believe, and how we act. Many are useful beliefs that drive personal values. Some are limiting beliefs that are a factor in keeping us stuck in non-productive behaviors. For example, if we think people don't like us, our defensive manner toward them could make this a reality. Henry Ford was correct when he said, *"If you think you can or think you can't, you're right."*

Components of Neuro-Linguistic Programming

Neuro – we create an individual world of reality through our senses;

Linguistic – represents the patterns we use to communicate with others and ourselves;

Programming – the way we organize our thinking and behaving in an attempt to get what we want.

The Useful Presuppositions Behind NLP

The Map is not the territory.

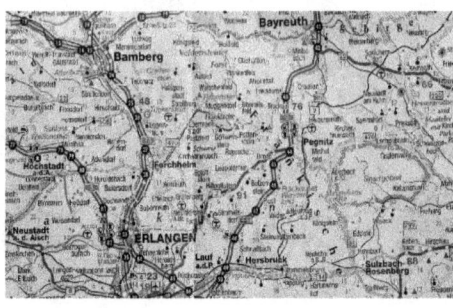

In the days before GPS, we consulted maps of places we wanted to go. That map, of course, was not the place itself. How we represent the world—our internal map—*refers* to reality; the map is not reality. How we think about the world, is not the world. We are responding to our perception of self, others, and the world that may or may not be correct. Gary used the metaphor of "writing on our walls" to recognize the impact of our life experiences on the decisions we make. No matter whether we or others in our life wrote on our "wall" we read and respond to those words as *our* reality.

People Work Perfectly.

No one is broken. People function perfectly, even if what they are doing is ruining their life. A goal for EFT is to find the experiences leading to self-sabotage. *Behavior is always valuable somewhere at some time. People make the best choice that they see available to them at any given time.* Put more simplistically—people are always doing the best they can. Our goal in relieving emotional distress is to add choices and increase client resources.

People have all the resources they need.

The term "resources" in NLP means the internal responses and external behaviors needed to get the desired response. Respecting that your *client does have within themselves the ability and resources to get what they* need, leads to their perception of more options. EFT practitioners help clear the blocks so they can recognize the resources and their options that are hidden within or to utilize resources and additional information others may offer. They can think more realistically, see more options, access more resources for dealing with their issue. Many times, our clients are *limited in their ability to see their alternatives,* options, and their internal and external resources. As I often put it:

If you don't see that you have an option, you don't have an option.*

The Meaning of Communication is the Response You Get.

The point of communication is to get an outcome—preferably the outcome you prefer. Effective communication is when you gain your desired outcome. All our verbal and non-verbal behaviors create a response. Every statement you make or action you take has a meaning to the recipient. As practitioners, we are constantly callibrating and assessing responses and modifying and adjusting as needed.

You Cannot *Not* Communicate.

We are always communicating—always—whether verbally, non-verbally, or behavioral. No response is still a response. In EFT, as in NLP, we carefully and consistently calibrate the response of the client and adjust our responses accordingly.

There is no Such Thing as Failure only Feedback.

Translated into an EFT session, all reports from the client give you information you can utilize to adjust or modify your approach. We tell clients there is no "wrong" answer; it is all feedback. Even if your statement or comment didn't "land," it gives you feedback as to what *not* to do and the incentive to find another path. You did not "fail," you gained another opportunity. Your goal now is to find the lesson or the opportunity exposed by the experience.

Mind and Body are Connected.

Our behavioral cues such as speech, tempo, breathing rate, even eye patterns reveal our internal sensory processing. This presupposition points out *the importance of calibrating* the client's responses. Our behaviors reflect the functioning of our mind; our body sensations reflect the emotions. It works the other way, as well. Exercising a particular behavior can affect the functioning of our mind and our emotions. For example, slumping in your chair can make you feel tired. Want to feel depressed? Go curl up in a fetal position in bed and cover your head with the blanket.

Every Behavior has a Positive Intent in Some Context.

No behavior is "wrong." All behavior is appropriate in some context or situation. Our goals in EFT are to find that context, those situations(s), creating the need for that behavior. All emotions are useful at some time, to protect us in some way or have someone to listen and understand. In EFT, we work to resolve the emotions around the event that created the decision to "behave" in a certain way. When emotions are calmed, we feel safer and able to modify our behavior. We see more options.

If it is Possible in the World, it is Possible for me.

Any skill, talent, or ability can be broken down into component steps and taught to anyone who does not have significant physiological or neurological damage. While it is true that we each have a unique brain that may make it easier or harder to do certain things, we often make a judgment about our ability to be successful after only limited effort. Telling ourselves, "I'm not any good at that," we give up too soon. We tend to see things as a whole rather than breaking them down into steps. It is certainly an effort to discover, study, and carry out the steps to accomplish something.

As practitioners, we help the client discover his or her resistance and reluctance that is keeping them from taking the "steps" toward their individual goal.

> **The Person or Element with the Most Flexibility in a System Will Have the Most Influence.**

The more options you see gives you more choices you have in how you could react. This is the "Law of Requisite Variety" from systems theory. *The one who sees the most options and can exercise a variety of behavioral choices has the upper hand in situations and negotiations.* The ability to respond to any situation in a variety of ways significantly improves your outcome. Any time you limit your behavioral choices or do not see your options and alternatives, you give others a competitive edge. This factor is another reason for *doing your own work.* You can better calibrate and respond to each individual in the most effective way when you've decreased your blind spots, developed more awareness of options and increased your ability to assess situations and react in a variety of ways.

NOTES

Credit:

*An Annism

Map photo by Thomas Kinto on Unsplash

Failure image is by Gerd Altmann on pixabay.com, modified in PowerPoint.

37

Guidelines for Thought Disorders

> **IN A NUTSHELL:** There is not much written about using EFT with more severe mental health disorders. This article shares a favorite part of the book, *The EFT Level 3 Comprehensive Training Resource*. Tracey Middleton, LCSW-C, worked with people who have psychotic disorders, and Dissociative Identity Disorder, formally known as Multiple Personality Disorder, *selectively* using EFT with marked benefits. She gives an excellent set of guidelines for this population.

Gary Craig often stated, "Don't go where you don't belong." Good advice! Tracey Middleton, however, has the training and experience to assess whether EFT is appropriate for each individual in her program. Since I worked with the more seriously mentally ill population for many years before EFT, I particularly admire the work she is doing and *the caution she is exhibiting.* Working with this population requires extra training, extra caution, and patience.

These guidelines from Tracey will be of help to qualified professionals considering using EFT with people having any psychotic or dissociative disorder. Realistically, EFT is *not always appropriate, or useful, and could be counter-productive* with this population. She offers excellent criteria to determine the appropriateness of EFT with this population.

Tracey writes: *"It is my responsibility as the Therapist to determine if using EFT as an alternative intervention is appropriate and safe for my client and that I have their permission to use it."* [Italics added for emphasis.] This can get complicated if my client is experiencing psychotic, delusional, and/or dissociative states. I have developed the following questions to help me discern this:

> **Working with this population requires extra training and extra caution.**

- Is the client able to **develop and articulate clear and concise goals** for using EFT? Can the client repeat back to you the goals of EFT as an intervention to demonstrate true understanding?

- Is the client able to **give informed consent** to the use of EFT on those specific issues and goals? Is the client able to understand its benefits, limitations, and possible abreactions? It is important to get the client's consent at different points in the session while using EFT. They may give consent to start using EFT and, in the middle of its application, decide to stop. Are you giving the client opportunities to change their mind and reassuring them that it is ok—whatever their decision?

- Is there a strong therapeutic alliance already established with the client that could tolerate a new intervention like EFT? Do you **know your client well enough to know when a yes to using EFT really means yes?** Some clients may say "yes" to EFT to please you, but really don't want to do it. This kind of interaction could lead to harm.

- Ask open-ended questions thoroughly to determine true consent. Have you assessed whether tapping on any of the acupoints might cause a stress response? Show the client a diagram with the EFT acupoints on it and **ask which points they would like to use** for EFT. Don't assume.

GUIDELINES FOR THOUGHT DISORDERS

- When using EFT as an intervention for those with delusions and/or auditory, visual, or olfactory hallucinations and/or dissociative states, it is important to assess **if the client is competent to consent** to their goals and possible benefits. If their goal is to reduce or stop delusions and/or hallucinations, can they verbalize and conceptualize what their life would be like without them? If they are unable to do this, it could increase the likelihood of abreaction and thus cause possible harm. **Author's note: If not, don't use EFT with that client at that time.**

- Does the **client have enough ego-strength* to adjust to the cognitive shifts** that come with EFT, or could the cognitive shifts cause decompensation in mental stability?

- Have you received **permission from your clinical supervisor** to use EFT with your client who has a severe chronic mental illness and discussed ways to decrease the likelihood of causing harm? Although EFT is an evidence-supported technique, there is limited research regarding its efficacy and limitations for the treatment of delusions, psychosis, hallucinations, and/or severe dissociative states.

Tracey goes on to say, "My experience has taught that if I can answer yes to the above questions, then I proceed to *use EFT on general and global symptoms*. Have the client use EFT on non-threatening issues FIRST to learn how it feels to use the technique and to become familiar with its benefits. Be sure to observe how the client responds to general cognitive shifts... see how EFT is tolerated. This will also allow more time for trust and rapport to develop between you and the client."

This is a particularly *challenging population to work with using any modality*. This is one of those areas where, *if you weren't qualified to work with them before EFT, you are not qualified to work with them with EFT*. Developing referral sources is an important responsibility for all EFT practitioners.

> **Use EFT on general and global symptoms.**

NOTES

*Ego-strength is used to describe individuals who can maintain their sense of identity and self in the face of adversity, distress, and conflict and can approach problems with the sense that he or she can not only overcome but also grow as a result. Low ego-strength refers to individuals who struggle to cope with problems, are overwhelmed by reality, and may avoid challenges and conflict. The term ego-strength comes from Freud's theory of personality, in which the personality is composed of three elements: the id, the ego, and the super-ego. Simply put, the id is comprised of primal urges and is present at birth. The super-ego is made up of standards and rules acquired from one's parents and society, and the ego is the part of the personality that mediates among the demands and standards of the id, the ego, the super-ego, and reality. Freud's understanding of personality, and how people think, is not considered as relevant in today's therapy world.

About the Books – *EFT Level 1 [& 2 & 3] Comprehensive Training Resource* books are just that: a comprehensive, well researched set of books that are a helpful compilation of EFT concepts and examples for using those concepts effectively and safely with others. They are invaluable for any serious student of EFT. Available on Amazon.com

38

Trivia – the eft

> **IN A NUTSHELL:** The letters EFT represent a real word, a proper noun with a totally different definition. The word "eft" is from the Old English word efeta, the name for the juvenile newt. In the biological world the eft, like our EFT, is all about transformation.

Meet Efeta - The red eft – Eft is an immature newt (Salamander), especially the reddish-orange terrestrial form of a North American species, and for you biologists out there the formal name is *Notophthalmus viridescens*.

These newts go from larva with gills living in the water, to eft the juvenile stage in which they lose their gills and travel distances over land. Like EFT, the eft works towards transformation, to "lose" what's no longer useful, to "grow" and "travel" to different "places" and gain new perspectives and new behaviors.

The aquatic larva stage, after hatching, lasts 2 to 5 months growing to about an inch before transforming into the terrestrial "eft" stage, spending its life on land.

This eft juvenile is a reddish-orange with two rows of black-bordered red spots. It has well-developed lungs, limbs, and eyelids – but no longer any gills. The eft acquires a bright orange-red coloration, beautiful but highly toxic.

Adult newts are yellowish-brown to greenish-brown and have black-bordered red spots. As an adult, it returns to the water to breed. This newt has the most complex and variable life history of any amphibian. It grows up to 5 inches and can live in the wild 12 to 15 years. Newts are popular aquarium pets.

The newt typically goes through four stages: egg, aquatic larva, eft, and terrestrial adult. But, also like our EFT clients, newts have individual variations in transitions; not all newts, or clients, go through all stages.

NOTES

Credits:

Image of newt eft, from "Hoarded Ordinaries" blog, www.hoardedordinaries.com by Dr.Lorianne DiSabato, taken August 6, 2006)

39

Another Bridge to EFT

> Perhaps your entire family accepts and encourages your journey into the alternative or energy world. My family, however, is more of the *just tolerating* kind. My sister, for instance, does not utilize any alternative therapy, and EFT is too "out there" for her. During one call, she was cautioning me that using EFT would make me less credible as a licensed professional.

Usually, I let such comments go by and stick to or stay with family topics, but that morning I had been listening to a presentation by Bruce Lipton. I launched in, "Well," I said, "I see it like this."

Scientists thought for a long time that genetics ruled our fate; that what we are born with is what we are stuck with. What scientists are finding is that the cells in our body respond to the environment they are put in, e.g., the chemicals in our blood. Chemicals that can make us feel good or feel bad; chemicals that help keep us healthy or contribute to illness or physical problems. If we can have some control over which set of chemicals being sent through our body, wouldn't we want to?

Our brain gives the signal to the body to release chemicals into our blood. Where does the brain get the information to decide to tell the body to release which chemical? From our senses—what we see, hear, smell, taste, sense, or feel. We have a thought that interprets what we've seen, heard, etc.—or at least what we *think* we've seen, heard, etc. Our thoughts are based on *our perception of what's happening* in our environment.

If our perception is positive, the brain signals the release of feel-good chemicals. When the perception is one of danger or negativity, our brain signals chemicals into our blood that, over time, can impact our body in negative ways, and can lead to illness, aches and pains, and diseases. I resist the idea that as we age, we are even more victims of our genes. I refuse to believe that we have no choice but to allow a past event to affect us adversely as if it were still happening today. When we've discovered ways that can neutralize the impact of our past negative experiences, shouldn't we use them?

This is not new stuff; we've known our genes responded to our environment since research from the late 1960s. We have also known for a long time that our emotions impact our health. It makes sense to address the negative experiences in our life that lead to negative thoughts and feelings that, over time, can lead to various physical challenges.

If we can modify the negative thoughts we are sending to our brain, the brain will send less "feel bad" chemicals. Resulting in a healthier environment for our genes, our cells, improving our chances for a healthier body. It's all tied together.

That is why I do what I do. I work to share with others a relatively simple tool that is effective in reversing the impact of negative thoughts and emotions. If we can decrease the negative, we have a much better chance of feeling happier and calmer and staying healthier longer with fewer aches and pains.

Granted, the above is an oversimplification; I suggest you read or listen to something by Bruce Lipton, but my sister gave a *rare* compliment. "That makes a lot of sense," she said, "You should write that down." So, I did.

There are many bridges to EFT, short and long. Just as using the client's language is an important part of successful rapport and outcome, so is using the language of your audience when discussing EFT.

When doing a very brief introduction to a newbie, I tie EFT into their awareness of the connections between body sensations and emotions. I may say,

> "We all have annoyances and negative memories of things that happen. When we think about these negative events, we have a physical sensation that shows up as a reaction in our body. We *cannot have an emotion without a body sensation;* that's how we know we have an emotion.
>
> EFT works to calm the body's response to the emotion, and, in doing so, the emotional response is decreased or eliminated. We all know that we *cannot be upset and calm at the same time.* EFT's job is to calm the body, so we can think more clearly and calmly about how to handle the problem. EFT uses some of the same points as acupuncture only we percuss, or tap, the points instead of using needles."

When I am marketing to a professional audience, I may say,

> "*EFT is a powerful stress management tool that decreases anxiety, increases body awareness, and encourages cognitive shifts.* EFT utilizes some of the same points used in acupuncture, we percuss or tap, instead of using needles. This process decreases or eliminates the physical sensations that are brought up by emotional distress, thereby decreasing or eliminating the emotion, often permanently."

AND, when talking to my relatives, all bets are off. I may, or may not, get further with more scientific-sounding stories along the lines of Bruce Lipton!

Resource: https://brucelipton.com

40

Support for Practitioners

> **IN A NUTSHELL:** While the practice of EFT is growing, it can still be hard to find other practitioners for support and community. One excellent resource for that support and community, and for increasing your EFT skills is the EFT Guild, an international EFT community-based in England with members from all over the world. Developed by Gwyneth Moss, EFT Founding Master, the EFT Guide represents "Quality, Clarity, Community."

The EFT Guild offers its members many opportunities to increase skills and effectiveness and to meet and benefit from other's experiences that are worth more—much more—than the minimal membership fee.

Open to all, whatever their route to learning EFT. The eftguild.org website states: *A guild is a supportive community of skilled craftspeople who join together to encourage learning and celebrate excellence. [The] EFT Guild offers practice and support, events, learning resources, and friendship.*

As a member, you can choose to participate in free

"daisy chains," EFT practice groups where you can find others to hone and practice your skills and meet people from all over the world. The site contains a treasure trove of quality articles, training courses, and audio and video recordings of EFT events. You can have your questions answered about anything EFT related, a complex case, a clarification, information on a topic. Also, members in the UK are eligible for discounted insurance. Whether just starting in your training in EFT or are an advanced practitioner., there is something for everyone.

Guild members offer Level 1, 2, and 3 classes and mentoring accepted for accreditation by EFTi. The Guild is an excellent resource for ongoing training on a variety of related and advanced topics.

Before 2020, the group helps an annual live EFT Gathering, now it is held online. One of the excellent presentations at the 2020 EFT Gathering was by Kris Ferraro, on addressing grief with EFT. Events are recorded and made available to members as part of their library.

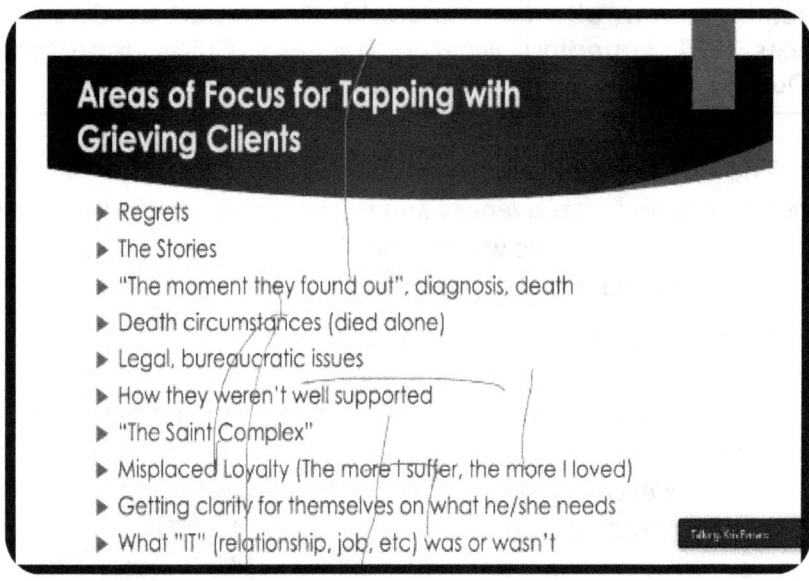

SUPPORT FOR PRACTITIONERS

Certification Bodies

There are a variety of for-profit groups offering EFT accreditation or certification, some of quality, and some not so much. There are only two not-for-profit groups, democratically run organizations, both established in 1999.

EFT International (EFTi) – Their website, EFTInternational.org, states it *"is committed to advancing and upholding the highest standards for education, training, professional development and promotion of the skillful, creative and ethical application of EFT worldwide."* Originating in the UK, EFTi has "policies and procedures in place to serve our members and safeguard the public."

They have clear guidelines for trainers who certify practitioners at various levels. EFTi also created an excellent Glossary of EFT terms. Google: EFT International Glossary of Terms. They also have a sign-up list for members to swap sessions.

2012 ACEP Conference * ACP-CEP graduates with Gary and Tina Craig

Association for Comprehensive Energy Psychology – Based in the United States, but with members all over the world. Their website states, *"ACEP is recognized as the largest international organization that promotes research and application of EP approaches, offering an indispensable network of resources for the public and media, a staunch advocate for members responsibly learning and applying EP models, and an influential presence helping shape mental health and healthcare practices."*

ACEP represents a *"family of integrative disciplines that apply energy-related concepts and models across multiple areas. There are both professional and lay disciplines under the ACEP umbrella that uniquely utilize this integrative approach in the healing and change process."*

ACEP currently offers two comprehensive training programs. One certifies practitioners in EFT, the other in Comprehensive Energy Psychology, which has one track for licensed mental health professionals and one for non-licensed practitioners. Read about both on their web site, energypsych.org, under the certification tab.

P.S.: There are other useful EFT sites, no way I can list them all, but one of my absolute favorites is a free weekly podcast on Gene Monterastelli's site, https://TappingQandA.com. You can access the archives for interviews with experts in EFT and other energy modalities. Gene is an excellent interviewer, chooses knowledgeable speakers, and covers useful and interesting topics. I'm even on there. *Podcast #218* discussing more effective ways to use EFT on your own.

NOTES

Credits:

EFT Guild web site: https://eftguild.org/

EFT International quotes from eftinternational.org

ACEP quotes from energypsych.org

Book image by congerdesign from Pixabay

Grief Slide by Kris Ferraro @ KrisFerraro.com

Group picture by another ACEP attendee.

Note: Tina left ACEP in 2015. She and Gary developed *Certification Program* for *The Gold Standard EFT. She ran this program until 2018 and has now moved on to other projects. The EFT tutorial remains on emofree.com and Gary holds classes now for Optimal EFT.

41

Self-Care Practices

> **IN A NUTSHELL:** The concept of self-care has exploded in the last few years. We are bombarded with ideas to "do this" or to "do that" to take care of ourselves. Some are time-consuming or unrealistic. Trying to work self-help exercises into your day can be exasperating. Ever had the thought, "You have got to be kidding! When do you expect me to work *that* into an already crowded day?" Micro-practices may be the answer for busy practitioners.

These final articles show some of the best of the simple, the short, the easy, the quick methods for self-care! We look at the *why* and some of the *how* of self-care and toss in some of my personal philosophy and practices that have kept and continue to keep me balanced.

Whatever your path, your journey, your timing, it is right for you now. Max Ehrmann, in his famous poem, Desiderata, encouraged everyone to "be gentle with yourself."

No one self-care practice best fits everyone. Each of us has our preferred way. Just like you respond to each individual as you assess and individualize what works for them, you evaluate and find self-care practices that work for *you*. Your self-care practices may change—probably should change—over time as you continue to increase your clarity, awareness, and empathy for yourself, others, and the world.

EFT IS SIMPLE—PEOPLE ARE COMPLEX

Everyone has their own path, their own journey, their own timing.*

Micro-practices

When I first heard about "micro-practices" practices from Ashley Davis Bush* that only take a minute—*really*, only a minute—I was immediately all ears. When she said there were three types of self-care—wait, I thought, that sounds more complicated, now I have to worry about three kinds!—but I persevered through my skepticism, and here's what I learned.

The three most common occupational stressors in the helping world are:

- Burn-out in which we need *relaxation*.

- Compassion fatigue when empathy flags, and we need

motivation and *energizing*.

- Trauma exposure, after which we need *grounding* to create our own safe harbor.

Bush created a list of three "short, simple, powerful" self-care exercises that could be completed quickly and for the most immediate impact. While we may be familiar with some of these, we may not have looked at these exercises from this perspective, and most of us probably don't use them!

Try to imagine yourself using each as you read through them. Better yet, take three minutes and practice each one.

- **Grounding:** Breath slowly for one minute—time it on your phone. On your in-breath think, *"I am calm."* On the out-breath, think, *"I am grounded."* [This is from One-Moment Meditation by Martin Boroson]** Author Note: Tapping while you do this works well.

- **Energizing:** Do one minute of Donna Eden's Cross Crawl, i.e., marching in place, knees high, arms swinging, crossing right elbow to the left knee, and left elbow to the right knee.

- **Relaxing:** Complete one minute of 4-7-8 diaphragmatic breathing. Inhale for a count of 4. Hold for a count of 7. Breathe out as through a straw for the count of 8. [From the EMDR protocol.]

Not sure which one you need at a particular point? Just do them all. The exercises are short, simple, and powerful. Mix them up, add EFT. *Wherever you are, whatever you are doing, whichever type of stress, give these three exercises a try.*

The following articles cover other short useful techniques I have personally found helpful. I challenge you to pick your favorites and practice every day for a month.

NOTES

* An Annism: Everyone has their own path, their own journey, their own timing.

EFT IS SIMPLE—PEOPLE ARE COMPLEX

Path Photo by Bryan Rodriguez on Unsplash

** Google One-Moment Meditation by Martin Boroson for short cute videos on quick meditation.

The information presented above is from an Ashley Davis Bush article in the Psychotherapy Networker. My favorite professional journal, always interesting stories, shares useful suggestions and is inexpensive for a professional journal. I highly recommend it to any practitioner, licensed or not.

Ashley Davis Bush also wrote Simple Self Care for Therapists, useful for all practitioners. Available from Amazon.com

42

Daily Tapping Routine

> **IN A NUTSHELL:** I added EFT to my self-care activities in 1999. I created a list of what I hoped would be a finite list and began tapping. I added to the list as I tapped; the items listed became smaller issues, but the list didn't seem to shorten much! Gary Craig set me straight when he told me *we are never through with all our issues*. I really didn't want to hear that! While the list did finally get shorter, I'd learned that my To-Tap list, like my To-Do list, would never be completed, that there will always be something.

The fact that we are never through is why we need a routine, a process, or a system for tapping with as much consistency as we can muster. Persistence and consistency are necessary for a practitioner. As we peel back those layers, we gain more awareness of our gaps and biases. We see more options available to us. We gain more ability to set our biases aside as we work with others for *their* highest and best interest. Note my choice of words: more awareness, more ability. We will *always* have gaps and biases. It comes with being human. *One hundred percent objectivity by any human is a myth.*

Over time we gain increasing awareness. With more awareness, we gain confidence and courage, and objectivity to be of greater service. While we are never finished, the list of events does not seem to be as emotionally overwhelming a task as when you began. But we can still be surprised. As we gain clarity, like on a hike through mountains, we conquer one peak only to realize there is another peak to climb that we could not see before.

After tapping for twenty years, I most often focus my morning tapping on three questions:

How's my breathing?

What is going on in my body right now?

What is my biggest challenge for the day?

I check my To-Tap list on an index card—which, btw, has room for ten items, quite enough of my "stuff" to look at and deal with at one time—thank you very much! The phrase "quality, not quantity" fits here. New problems, new aspects, and deeper issues continue to appear.

Like most of you practitioners and entrepreneurs out there, I am busy. I only tap a few minutes a day. Sometimes issues that come up take several days to address. I jot the event(s) or aspect(s) on an index card,* to address the next day.

First, I check my breath. *What percent of a full breath am I taking today?* Breath is often our early warning system. I tap until it is up to 100%, or as far as it will go, or something else pops up I need to address.

What is going on in my body today? How am I feeling? I tap for whatever uncomfortable physical feelings I may have right in that moment.

What is the biggest issue today that brings up a negative emotion? I look at whatever problem is in-my-face at the time. Keeping down overwhelmed is an on-going battle for most entrepreneurs. At times I use my tapping buddies to work through what's behind the problem and the best approach for whatever is facing me. Since you cannot have an emotion without a corresponding body sensation, I always start by addressing the body sensation.

Ever noticed how most things that annoy or frustrate us are about what someone *did, or didn't do,* something that we think *they should have done or should not have done.* Sometimes that "someone" is us.

We can often track upsets to earlier experiences. Granted, there are people and things in this world that are indeed annoying. Not only will we never finish clearing all our stuff, but we also will never run out of annoying people and things in our life.

Tapping down the list forces me to deal with *what it is about me* that the issue or the person brings up. Trust me, it is motivating to stop being so annoyed with people if every time you get annoyed at someone else's behavior and after tapping for the issue, you realize you are looking at some expression of that behavior in yourself! Confronting my ego and pettiness makes it easier to practice my belief that *everyone is doing the best they can to get what they want, to meet their needs at that time*—even if I think what they are doing is not in their self-interest *or mine.* If someone saw a better option for themselves, they would have done something else. Which leads to the Annism,

> **If you don't see you have an option, you do not have an option.***

Which leads to another Annism: if you feel bad that you still have so many "issues" and think you see others who seem to have it all together, trust me,

> **If you think someone has it all together, you just don't know them well enough!**

Do I *always* tap every day? No. I am human, with all the corresponding foibles that go along with our species. I've been known to go spells without tapping at all!! But don't tell anyone.

NOTES

*TRIVIA: I am a big fan of 3X5 index cards. Back in what is considered prehistoric times by today's college students, index cards held my notes and quotes to arrange for typing. And—really showing my age—typed my papers on a manual typewriter. I was excited to inherit an electric typewriter from an outgoing student! A huge improvement for completing my thesis, but still, no spell check or easy rearranging or deleting like our computers of today.

43

Using Pre-sleep Moments

> **IN A NUTSHELL:** Sleep is a challenge for many—including me sometimes. I have been a fan of Wayne Dyer's approach since his first book in 1976. Excerpts from one of his many blogs, "How Do You Sleep?" suggests we use our pre-sleep moments to prime our brain not only for sleep but to ensure a positive outlook for the next day.

> I am peaceful, I am content, I am love.

Dr. Dyer says, *"the last thought you have in your mind* [before sleep] *can last up to four hours in your subconscious mind. That's four hours of programming from just one moment of contemplation before going into your unconscious state."*

To assure his sleep *"will be dominated by* [his] *last waking concept of* [himself], Dyer states a series of "I am" statements. *"I am peaceful; I am content, I am love, I am writing, I am the governing power of the universe, and I attract to myself only those who are in alignment with my highest ideals of myself."*

He says that you can use those pre-sleep moments either review the *"unhappy, frustrated, and anxious"* thoughts or you can decide to "program your subconscious mind with thoughts of joy, kindness, gratitude, and anticipation of having your wishes *fulfilled."*

If you are unable to program your thoughts to the positive, get out of bed. Dyer suggests, *"take a few deep breaths, read from a spiritual text, meditate for a few moments in front of a white candle, say a prayer, do anything other than stay lying down. You cannot defend yourself against these onslaughts while remaining snug in your bed."*

Wayne Dyer became a tapper later in life; if he had written that blog today, he would have added EFT to the list. Perhaps he would have suggested to use very light taps or to hold the points gently as you take a breath, or to imagine tapping the points, or to tap for the body sensations of what is bothering you, without words.

In the morning, Dr. Dyer believes what happens that day *"is essentially predetermined by my feelings as I prepared for sleep, and while I was in that place of warmth and trust in the arms of the one universal subconscious mind."*

Dr. Dyer suggests you post by your bed and read each night, a mantra: **"Good things are going to happen."** Turning off our busy brains before we sleep can be a challenge. Giving it something else to do helps. Give it a try.

NOTES

Credit:

Candle photo by Hans Vivek on Unsplash

For more ideas that can improve your life see: www.DrWayneDyer.com.

44

What is Your Talisman?

> **IN A NUTSHELL:** I first met Lulu when traveling in New Zealand in 2010 where I was invited to teach EFT. Lulu became a talisman for me. Throughout history, people have created meaningful symbols and objects that remind and inspire and encourage. In Lulu's case, she is a *reminder for me, to-get-on-with-it with grace and confidence.*

I was thrilled to visit New Zealand! I was invited by Ruth Ross, a counselor at a mental health clinic in Dunedin, who I had mentored for the DCEP program with ACEP. I rented an RV for five weeks to travel to EFT classes in three cities, and, of course, to see the beautiful country. It was a wonderful experience and a joy to meet such warm and friendly people and so many dedicated NZ EFTers. The second class was in Palmerston North, sponsored by EFT Master and psychotherapist, Barbara Smith,* who was responsible for much of the spread of EFT in New Zealand. The third, in Auckland, with Liz Hart, EFT coach.

It was a lovely and memorable trip. Sightseeing on the drive to Dunedin, I stopped in Christchurch. There, in the gift shop of the beautiful Christchurch Cathedral (pre-earthquake), sat Lulu. It was love at first sight. We've been together ever since.

EFT IS SIMPLE—PEOPLE ARE COMPLEX

Let me introduce Lulu:

– *a very*

– *small*

– *stuffed*

– *lamb.*

When I left New Zealand, I brought Lulu home. Taking future trips, long or short, in my 19-foot RV, sometimes with a friend, but always with my dog Morkie, my GPS Tommie—and Lulu.

Why Lulu?

Originally, having Lulu on the NZ trip in the RV was simply a lark. She had a place to sit to see the sites and a slot in the dash for a little bed. When Lulu came home with me, she sat on my desk, originally merely as a souvenir. I'd look up at her and smile at the memory of the terrific trip. Over time, however, as she sat patiently through more projects and events, Lulu evolved to become my talisman, *my token for grace under pressure.* Lulu is a reminder that whatever happens, I can deal with it. I may not like it, I may be upset for a while, it may take a long time, I may have to tap, but I can deal with it.

One day when I'd just finished a large project and needed a shift in focus, I looked up, and there, with her steady presence was Lulu. On the spot, I decided to write a dedication to Lulu. Why a dedication to a stuffed—but very cute—little lamb? Not only for my joy in completing a huge task—but as *a thank you to the characteristics* Lulu represents. Lulu is my reminder that *"OK, it's a challenge, you've handled challenges before; this is doable, take it a step at the time. Get on with it."*

Silly? Should I have picked a more grownup image? Maybe. Isn't the injunction to put away childish things? But isn't it the child in us that becomes afraid? The child in us that worries about

WHAT IS YOUR TALISMAN?

managing the world. Lulu became my symbol of confidence in accomplishment. Lulu is my reminder, my anchor, of my ability to *get on with it*. Sometimes I really need that! Sometimes I think we all need that.

Don't worry. Lulu doesn't work all the time. Here is Lulu, relaxing after a hard day in the office.

Throughout time people have given significant meaning to symbols. Your talisman, your symbol, for *I-can-do-it-get-on-with-it* is probably very different from mine. A symbol from which you draw inspiration and confidence.

Lulu was there as well for the editing of this book.

Lulu says, "Wow, that was a lot of work. We think it turned out OK, and that you'll find it useful. Thanks for reading."

Below is the dedication to Lulu; *a dedication to all positive symbols – and people – that encourage me to keep-on-keeping-on in the face of challenge and adversity.*

Dear Lulu, Thank you for your patience, your constant presence, and quiet acceptance during so many challenging events and times and projects. Thank you for being a powerful reminder that I-can-do-it-get-on-with-it. Thank you for reminding me too that there can be grace under pressure, no matter how upsetting or annoying things can be. I am grateful for the meaning and encouragement you represent in my life.

Postscript: The 2011 earthquake in Christchurch, New Zealand, killed 185 people and destroyed many buildings and homes in and around the city, including the collapsing of the Christchurch Cathedral spire. Lulu's original "home" in the church gift shop was no more. Our hearts went out to, and still go out to, all those in Christchurch and all New Zealand.

NOTES

*Barbara Smith, EFT Founding Master, died in her sleep on August 13, 2019. She had been in a memory care home for the last several years with Alzheimer's. Dedicated to EFT, she continued using EFT to help other residents. Barbara was a generous, kind, and loving person who will be missed.

Credit:
Photos of Lulu by Author

45

Hardwiring Happiness

> **IN A NUTSHELL:** This is one of those little gems that may help make self-care a bit more fun. Your client may like it as well. If you read any spiritual literature, you've gotten the message in a variety of ways to "practice gratitude." Great idea, easier said than done. Our brain seems to focus on and remember more negative than positive. Fortunately and unfortunately *the more we focus, the more what we focus on is installed.*

We do tend to appreciate the highlights in life, but we often ignore or pass by the multiple positive little things that happen throughout our day—the small things we take for granted. If we *should* happen to notice, we tend to give it little attention. Rick Hanson, a neuropsychologist and an authority on happiness, shared ideas in a NICABM recording, as to how to hold on to and instill positive emotions. He says we need to *focus on the positive long enough for our brain to install it—and this absorption takes only 12 seconds!* You may, or may not, realize how long 12 seconds can seem when you are working to

focus on a positive feeling. A mere 12 seconds can feel like a very long time.

Whatever the intensity of the feeling, mild or strong, the goal is to *"intend and sense" that positive feeling—and absorb it into you like water into a sponge.* Hanson shares a creative way to use those 12 seconds to absorb the positive feeling. He suggests you *create an imaginary Treasure Chest in your heart.* Imagine you are *placing a jewel of your choice in the chest with each positive,* however small.

Metaphors are useful, and it sounded like a fun idea. That night, feeling cozy in my comfortable bed, I created my Treasure Chest, and in gratitude for my bed, placed my first jewel. The next morning, I woke up. Waking up is worthy of a beautiful jewel. My feet and legs still worked when I got out of bed. A ruby this time. The light switch turned the lights on. The colors of the sky added a handful of tiny rainbow jewels. Morkie, my dog, "saying" good morning, the stove heated the water for the tea; the orange juice cold, I had a closet full of clothes to pick from; my car started in the cold; a nice email from a friend; my neighbor waved at me. Lots of opportunities to add a jewel.

My intent for the day was to notice anything even minutely positive. Checking my Treasure Chest at the end of the day, there were lots of jewels large and small but plenty of room for more. I realized *there was unlimited space. We could never overfill our Treasure Chest.*

NOTES

Credit: Book photo from Amazon. Treasure chest photo by Jouwen Wang on unsplash.com

46

Motivating Literature

> **IN A NUTSHELL:** Many roads lead to self-esteem, a positive sense of our self-worth. While EFT is a useful tool for resolving our negative beliefs about self, others, and the world there are many paths to "enlightenment." Reading can influence our perceptions, inspire an ah-ha moment, or give us the motivation to finally, finally change something in ourselves. *Literature can help reframe our views of ourselves, others, and the world.* We may decide to take better care of our amazing mind and body, to see ourselves as the imperfect but perfect humans we are, and to create a more fulfilling life.

Motivating literature does not have to be classic literature. Indeed, it can be as simple as a throwaway sentence in a novel that gives us that ah-ha moment in which we are forever changed. Books and poetry have always been an important part of my life, often opening up a path to explore, showing options I had not previously noticed, introducing perspectives I hadn't considered.

Invictus, by William Henley, is a source of inspiration. *Desiderata* is a symbol of fortitude, I remain grateful to its author, Max Ehrmann. The *Serenity Prayer* and the *Lord's Prayer* have been inspirational for my life since the challenging teenage years, long before I learned EFT. And then there is DLB493 to put annoying situations in perspective. (Read on). I still treasure them all.

Since my youth, the philosophy in *Invictus* has been a goal to strive toward. I am unable to say that I have conquered the "not winced nor cried aloud" section or never "bowed" to the pain. Some pains were too much for me to bear silently. I can say that I consider myself the master of my fate and the captain of my soul. I believe that how my life turns out is, in most part, up to me. None of us control, nor can we ever control, everything that happens to us. The focus of this poem is how we deal with what happens. I believe that I am responsible for *how I deal* with what happens. Sometimes, dealing with the issue means seeking help from others, and sometimes *dealing* can take a while.

Invictus

Out of the night that covers me,
Black as the pit from pole to pole,
I thank whatever gods may be
For my unconquerable soul.

In the fell clutch of circumstance
I have not winced nor cried aloud.
Under the bludgeoning of chance
My head is bloody but unbowed.

Beyond this place of wrath and tears
Looms but the Horror of the shade,
And yet the menace of the years
Finds and shall find me unafraid.

It matters not how strait the gate,
How charged with punishments the scroll,
I am the master of my fate:
I am the captain of my soul.

William Ernest Henley, 1875

MOTIVATING LITERATURE

Desiderata

Go placidly amid the noise and haste,
and remember what peace there may be in silence.
As far as possible without surrender
be on good terms with all persons.
Speak your truth quietly and clearly;
and listen to others,
even the dull and the ignorant;
they too have their story.

Avoid loud and aggressive persons,
they are vexations to the spirit.
If you compare yourself with others,
you may become vain and bitter;
for always there will be greater and lesser persons than yourself.
Enjoy your achievements as well as your plans.

Keep interested in your own career, however humble;
it is a real possession in the changing fortunes of time.
Exercise caution in your business affairs;
for the world is full of trickery.
But let this not blind you to what virtue there is;
many persons strive for high ideals;
and everywhere life is full of heroism.

Be yourself.
Especially, do not feign affection.
Neither be cynical about love;
for in the face of all aridity and disenchantment
it is as perennial as the grass.

Take kindly the counsel of the years,
gracefully surrendering the things of youth.
Nurture strength of spirit to shield you in sudden misfortune.

But do not distress yourself with dark imaginings.
Many fears are born of fatigue and loneliness.
Beyond a wholesome discipline,
be gentle with yourself.

You are a child of the universe,
no less than the trees and the stars;
you have a right to be here.
And whether or not it is clear to you,
no doubt the universe is unfolding as it should.

Therefore be at peace with God,
whatever you conceive Him to be,
and whatever your labors and aspirations,
in the noisy confusion of life keep peace with your soul.

With all its sham, drudgery, and broken dreams,
it is still a beautiful world.
Be cheerful.
Strive to be happy.

Max Ehrmann, 1927

As long as I have had a desk, the Serenity Prayer was posted above it. I continue to struggle with the "wisdom" part of the prayer. I still repeat this prayer, particularly when I am frustrated at things not going the way I want them to or think they ought to.

The Serenity Prayer

God, grant me the Serenity to accept the things I cannot change, the courage to change the things I can, and Wisdom to know the difference.

I was taught The Lord's Prayer as a child and have repeated it countless times. In 2002, I took a trip to Virginia Beach to Edgar Casey's A.R.E. Library (Association for Research and Enlightenment.) Both the beach and the museum were beautiful and both a fascinating and memorable adventure—including the seagull relieving himself on my favorite jacket.

A guide for the museum said that *each word of the Lord's Prayer vibrates in ways that help to balance our energy* and therefore calm the body.

Like many other things, this information makes me wonder. The Lord's Prayer was not originally written in English. Are the vibrations the same in another language? Whether it "vibrates" or not, throughout my life I've used the Lord's Prayer to calm myself. In high school, I remember during difficult times hiding in the bathroom and repeating the Lord's Prayer over and over.

At the first EFT Master Showcase, 2006, in Dallas, Texas, I was nervous, not only was I responsible for all the planning, getting the presenters and participants, paying the bills, etc. Gary Craig was in attendance! I was in charge; I was the "master of ceremonies," I felt the heavy burden. Just before we were to begin, I grabbed a few minutes alone. Did I tap? Here I was organizing a tapping event with lots of EFTers there. I'd been tapping for seven years by then and certainly had tapped during all the planning, etc. At that moment, however, I didn't even think about tapping. Nope, I fell back on the tried and true: I repeated The Lord's Prayer out loud twice. Perhaps the words really do have vibrations that work to calm our body.

The Lord's Prayer

Our Father, which art in heaven,
Hallowed be thy Name.
Thy Kingdom come.
Thy will be done in earth,
As it is in heaven.
Give us this day our daily bread.
And forgive us our trespasses,

EFT IS SIMPLE—PEOPLE ARE COMPLEX

As we forgive those that trespass against us.
And lead us not into temptation,
But deliver us from evil.
For thine is the kingdom,
The power, and the glory,
For ever and ever.
Amen.

Matthew 6:9–13 King James version

I would be remiss if I didn't share a phrase that has also been beneficial in my life in dealing with frustrations and annoyances generally initiated by something someone did or didn't do, that I felt they should have or should not have done.

This little sign helped me assess whose problem is whose. Was it my problem, in which I needed to take some action to resolve, or if it was not my problem and out of my ability to "fix," to then "accept what I cannot change?" It prevented me from feeling a victim.

Years ago, working in a tough job with difficult people, I placed an index card on my wall stating only: DLB493. It was a code for "Non carborundum illegitimi," a faux Latin phrase meaning, "Don't let the bas...ds grind you down." I used the format of a Georgia state vehicle tag. DLB stood for the first of the phrase, the 493 from the phone for the last part.

DLB493

I never told anyone what it stood for! When I was annoyed or frustrated, I'd look up at DLB493, decide whose problem it was. Do what I could, then I'd smile at my little joke and get on with my day.

Trivia: Carborundum is a silicon carbide stone, an abrasive for grinding. The phrase is said to be initiated by the British lower-ranked soldiers during World War II. Noli pati a scelestis opprimi is the genuine Latin phrase.

*More Trivia: At the time I created the DLB493 code, the phones were still "dialed" to place a call. If you are young enough to have never used a phone with a circular dial, you may wonder why the number pad on the current phone does not follow the number pad for calculators? By beginning with the buttons with the number 1, made the new number pad for phones follow the order of the numbers on the now very old-fashioned dial phones. The goal, I suppose, was to make it an easier transition to a new way of operating the telephone.

APPENDIX 1

EFT Level 1 and 2
Training Review

EFT Level 1 and 2 Training Review

INTRODUCTION

The purpose of this brief review of a Level 1 and 2 Class is four-fold:

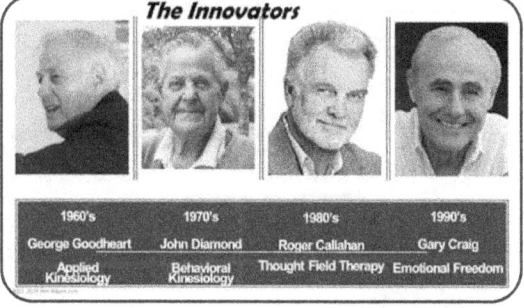

- to give a brief summarization of topics covered in your recent EFT classes,
- to assist you in taking the EFT International (EFTi) Level 2 exam,
- to introduce advanced EFT topics, and
- to point out the differences between EFTi Guidelines and

Gary Craig's Gold Standard EFT. EFTi modifications are minor and based on experience and feedback from hundreds of practitioners. However, as an EFT practitioner, you should understand the differences.

Repetition is an important part of the learning of any new skill. If you are a serious student of EFT planning to take an exam for accreditation, other helpful resources are:

1) EFT Level 1 (and 2) Comprehensive Training Resource books. Useful also for experienced practitioners, I highly recommend them – even if I am a co-author! The books are well-researched and written specifically to be an additional complement to EFT classes. EFT International (and other accreditation/certification programs) recommends these books as well.

2) The EFTi Glossary of Terms gives a clarifying definition for each EFT technique, and

3) Take a **second Level 2 class** with a different instructor.

STANDARD EFT PROTOCOL

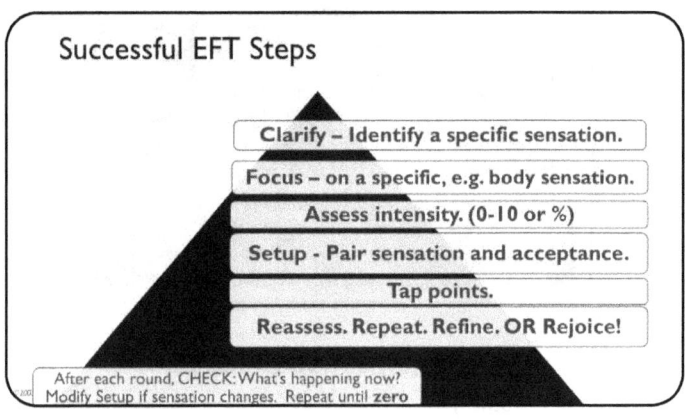

The EFT protocol:

- **Clarifying** what to address.

- Deciding upon the **focus.**

- **Assessing** the intensity, generally using a 0 to 10 scale.

- **Developing and Stating a Setup**, i.e., joining a self-acceptance statement with the focus and stated as you tap on the fatty side of the hand, repeating one to three times.

- **Tapping** the sequence of points as you state a Reminder Phrase, using keywords with the client's words.

- **Reassess the intensity. Test the results** of the tapping and refine or modify the focus on the problem if necessary.

Often clients present with a general or global issue or a limiting belief that is creating a challenge in their life. Initially, they may not know what is behind their challenge. We establish rapport and gain an understanding of their "frame" of the world, their presenting problem, and their goals. We may begin by approaching a more global problem or general description of the issue *to narrow down* to specific events behind the problem, and to decrease intensity and reluctance to addressing the problem directly. We help the client find and address the experience(s) that led to the decision, belief, or behavior behind their problem.

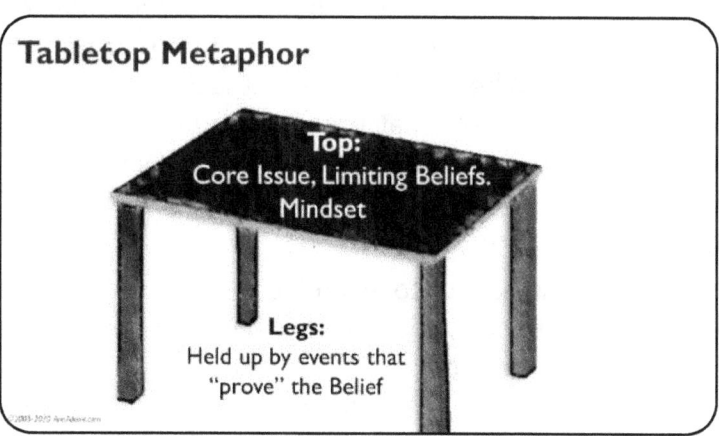

Gary Craig used Robert Cialdini's metaphor of a **Tabletop** to represent a **core issue**, i.e., a limiting belief or mindset behind the problem. Our core issues, the limiting beliefs about ourselves, others, and the world, generally show up as definitive statements or negative self-judgments leading to self-sabotaging behaviors.

Examples would be: I always, I never, I must, others are always

___, everything I do is wrong, I'll never get ahead, I am not good enough to ___, everyone should ___, people like me can't ___, all of [this/them] are ___, nobody ___, everyone___, etc.

Beliefs that restrict our lives in various ways are often given to us by an "authority" figure, sometimes even before we have language, perhaps before we were born. These beliefs may operate as the 11th commandment for their life. Beliefs show up as the words we choose, the attitudes, behaviors, and opinions we share. Watch for their **Tail Enders**, those yes-buts, the negative or self-limiting, often conflicting, comments about themselves.

Tabletops represent the decisions formed and perceptions of self, others, and the world. Events that back up or "prove" the belief and create the **Legs** that support the Tabletop. Events are composed of details or aspects that show up in the answers to who, what, when, where, how, and include information from the five senses: what you saw, heard, smelled, tasted, and any related tactile sensation. *Emotions around those details show up as body sensations.*

We are most helpful to our clients when we help **narrow the problem to a specific event, time, place, thing, or person.** Use questions such as: Where did you learn that? Do you remember when you realized that? What proof do you have of that? How does that show up as a problem? When was the last time that was a problem? What is your theory about this? What do you most want from this session?

Practitioners work to uncover and resolve or reframe problematic beliefs that underpin much of our day to day reactions and behaviors. We find and resolve the events from which the core issue/belief was formed. Fortunately, the concept of **Generalization** helps, since after addressing a few events or details, related "legs," holding up our "Tabletop" issue, can collapse as well, resolving our issue and allowing for a new perspective.

After the client reports zero intensity, we test our results by "replaying" the event searching for any residual emotions, checking for any intensity, or remaining aspect or detail. We want to assure the complete resolution of underlying events.

Moving from the **global to a specific event** and addressing the aspects can take time and detective work. Ask "investigative reporter" questions, who, what, when, where, how, what body sensations, and which five senses are involved, to uncover events, aspects, or details. Persistence is often necessary for the resolution of the complex issues involved. Additional sessions may be needed to address multiple events thoroughly. *One-minute wonders are rare.*

Writing on Your Walls is used as a metaphor to explain how we, and others in our life, "write" messages on the internal "walls" that impact what we believe and how we perceive ourselves, others, and the world. We consult those "walls" frequently reinforcing and holding those negative beliefs in place.

Setup – After developing rapport, clarifying the issue to be addressed, **assessing the intensity,** generally using a 0 to 10 scale with 10 being the most intensity, you then establish a **Setup**, a two-part statement of the issue/event/aspect to be addressed, and a positive, accepting statement. The default, "I deeply and completely accept myself" is often used. However, any positive acceptance statement will work. A statement that the client chooses that truly fits what the client believes may bring even more benefit, e.g. I'm OK, I'm a good person, I dared to come here, I like myself, I might think about someday accepting myself, etc.

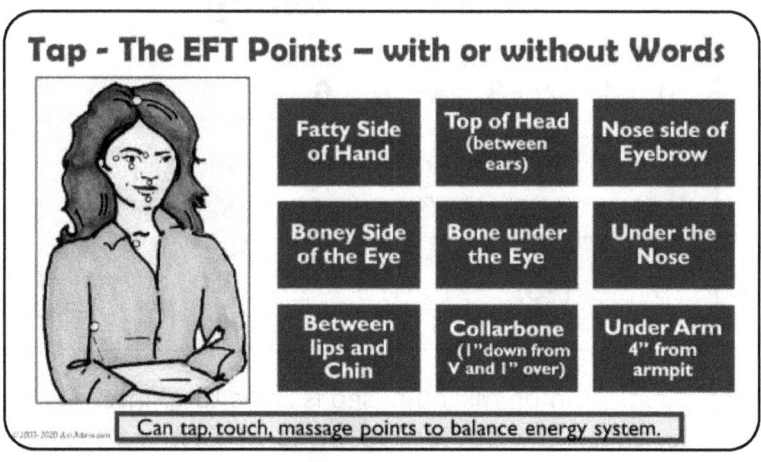

The Points – the **Setup is stated** as you are tapping on the fatty side of the hand (SOH) point. *The term Karate Chop point is no longer used to refer to the side of the hand.* Then, using some of the client's words as a **Reminder Phrase,** you tap the remaining points in an easy-to-remember, down-the-body manner: head, eyebrow, side of the eye, under-eye, under the nose, chin, collarbone, underarm. The actual order of points is not important and could be tapped in any order. Some clients may notice that **one point** seems more responsive than other points.

Measuring and Testing – We test for initial intensity before tapping and afterward to assess progress, or lack thereof, during a session. Testing gives feedback as to the direction of the next Setup and assesses when an issue, aspect, or event is resolved.

There are numerous ways to test our results. Intensity levels (0 to 10), percentages, outstretched or raised and lowered hands. In some cases when someone can't/won't/doesn't relate to numbers they can use words such as a lot, some, a little, none or small, medium, large, or how close or far away it seems, or temperature, or colors. Occasionally the Validation of Cognition Scale **(VoC)**, numbers 1-7, and is used to measure the strength of a belief to give the choice of a middle number. *Any measure of variation meaningful to the client will work.*

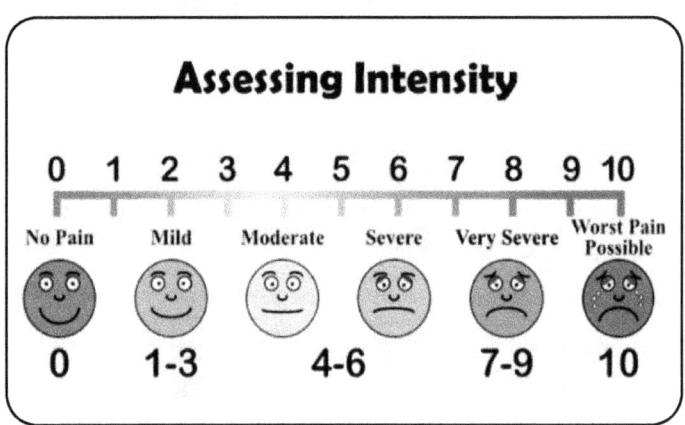

The most common method used is the 0 to 10 intensity scale. This scale, called the **Subjective Units of Distress Scale,** was adapted from one developed by Joseph Wolpe in 1969, to track progress using cognitive-behavioral treatments for anxiety disorders and research. Often abbreviated SUD, SUDS, or SUDs, it is seen frequently in EFT literature or on websites discussing EFT. However, it is *not necessary to teach this term to your clients;* after all, we are to follow their words, *not* teach them unnecessary new words.

Investigate the event by asking clarifying questions to uncover related events and aspects. Assess intensity after each round or shift of aspect. When intensity is reported to be zero, test the results by going back over the situation trying to bring up any remaining bits of intensity or aspects not yet addressed. Try to **vividly imagine** the situation, exaggerate the sights, sounds, etc. Or **role-play** the event or simulate a future experience. The *ultimate test is to assess the impact in real life,* **in vivo** *testing.*

Since you may address several events during a session, go back at the end of the session to assess what progress there was on the initial presenting problem. The best measure of resolution, certainly the most satisfying, is when the client shifts their perspective, creates a **cognitive shift,** for their issue.

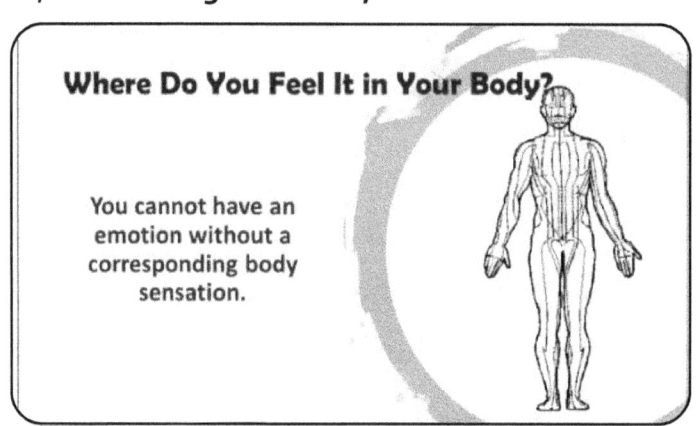

Where Do You Feel It in Your Body?

You cannot have an emotion without a corresponding body sensation.

Flexibility *for meeting client needs is more important* than always following every instruction to the letter. However, a thorough grounding in the EFT process is important; learn the rules before you break the rules! At Level 2, you are still learning to be proficient in using the EFT tools with a variety of clients.

Body Sensations – There has been significantly more emphasis and focus on body sensations and toward caution and safety for clients as we learn more about addressing the impact of trauma. Addressing body sensations can help the client ease into difficult aspects of past events. The Mantra still holds:

> **For results that are terrific, it helps to be specific.** **

A body sensation is a specific detail and is representative of the emotion itself. The body sensation *is* the emotion. As you calm the sensation, you calm the emotion, and at the same time, the intensity around the aspect or issue is decreased or resolved. As an added benefit you increase body awareness. Some clients are so out of touch with their bodies and emotions that you may have to teach them how to feel their bodies. The question, where do you feel that in your body as you talk about that, is appropriate as a part of any EFT Technique.

EFT techniques were developed to help prevent severe reactions to trauma by moving gently and slowly into the issue one small piece at the time. The goal is to "sneak up" on issues to be as painless as possible. Your approaches will vary with the client's needs.

> **The EFT process can be simple—focus, and tap—but people can be very complex.** **

THE EFT TECHNIQUES

The Narrated Movie Technique – While the EFTi recognizes Craig's original **Movie Technique** and **Tell the Story** as separate techniques, the EFTi Glossary states that the Movie and the Story "are nuanced—not everyone will facilitate it or walk through it in quite the same way." The concepts can now be taught together. However, many trainers and practitioners still use the Movie Technique and Tell the Story as separate techniques. A summary steps for the Narrated Movie Technique are to

- ▶ Pick a short moment in time that has a beginning, middle, and end, less than 2 minutes.
- ▶ Pick a non-triggering title for the "movie" [author note, ask for the first title that pops in their mind to help prevent going "into" the issue.]

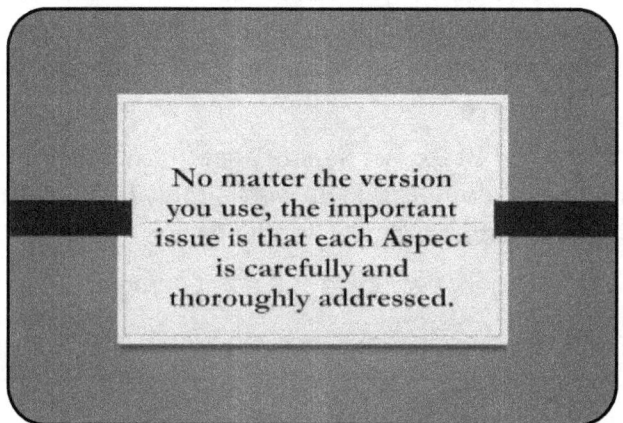

No matter the version you use, the important issue is that each Aspect is carefully and thoroughly addressed.

- ▶ Assess intensity
- ▶ Tap only for the title before getting into details.
- ▶ Assess intensity when as low as it will go, four or less.
- ▶ Begin addressing the details of the "movie."
- ▶ "Run the movie" or narration of the event.
- ▶ Stop at each point of even minor intensity.
- ▶ Assess intensity, when zero,
- ▶ Test the results by vividly imagining the scene, role-playing a future similar event, or, if you are able, check it out in vivo, a real-life trial.

Caution: As always, whenever the intensity is six or above, work to reduce intensity before going to any specific. Encourage the use of all five senses when "running" the movie silently, e.g., notice what you see, what you hear, are there any tactile aspects, are there any smells or tastes involved, what body sensations do you feel?

EFT IS SIMPLE—PEOPLE ARE COMPLEX

Movie Differences – Gold Standard EFT tutorial differentiates between the **Movie Technique** and **Tell the Story**. Many practitioners still use and teach the Movie and Tell the Story techniques as separate techniques. The emofree.com tutorial states that the Movie Technique begins by imagining the event silently, without sharing the details verbally. Whether called a "movie" or a "video clip," it is a metaphor designed to distance the emotional impact. The later steps for the Movie Technique are similar to Tell the Story.

Tell the Story Steps – The story method begins by verbally sharing the event almost as if you were simply telling it to a friend. Assess intensity, address anxiety about telling the story.

- Start the story *beginning* at a point *before the* event.

- Encourage the client to stop at *any,* even mild, intensity.

- Continue to the end of the story, continuing to stop to tap for any aspect bringing any intensity.

- Then repeat the story until *no* intensity on any detail or aspect.

- Test using **Vivid Visualization,** i.e., make the aspects closer, brighter, louder, more exaggerated.

- Tap for any remaining intensity.

- Test "in vivo," i.e., a real-life situation when possible.

Important similarity: Each version recognizes the importance of *step-by-step handling of all the activated aspects of the event.* Assess intensity, address the fear of "going there," address aspects of the event one by one, and encourage the client to stop at *any* level of intensity.

Chasing the Pain — Tap on whatever *physical sensations or symptoms* are experienced, modifying wording as the sensation changes, e.g., the intensity goes up or down, moves or a new symptom arises or a change in the quality of the sensation/symptom. *Using a metaphor* for the sensation or issue is effective and can be considered a gentle or distancing technique as well. *Use investigative questions* to help identify any emotional drivers. EFT relaxes the body and frees stuck energy to enable the body to use its healing wisdom. EFT does *not* cure any illness or disease.

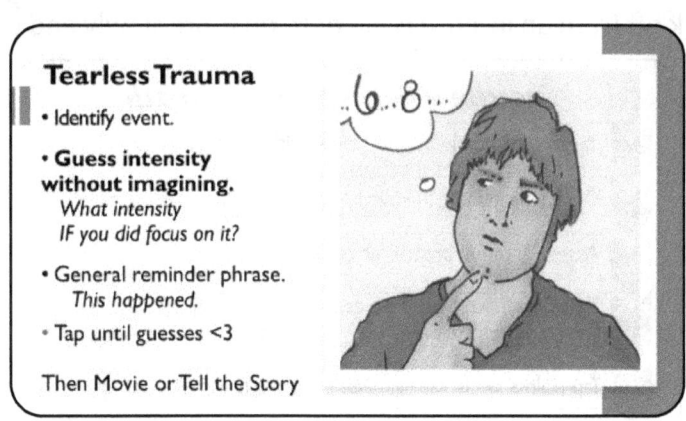

Tearless Trauma
- Identify event.
- **Guess intensity without imagining.** What intensity IF you did focus on it?
- General reminder phrase. *This happened.*
- Tap until guesses <3

Then Movie or Tell the Story

Tearless Trauma Technique — (TTT) ask the client to give an immediate guess as to what the intensity would be *if* they were to focus on the event. TTT is a gentle technique offering **protective distancing** or "disassociation" from a painful event until they are more comfortable in addressing it directly. Useful with potentially high-intensity events that you/they know would be very upsetting.

Ask them to give a one or two-word generic title such as, "This Happened," or "The Big One," or "The Green Door," "Angry man," etc. Tap for the title until the guessed intensity is three or below. Use any version of Movie or Tell the Story, addressing each detail as it arises. Slow down or back up to use a distancing or calming method if intensity escalates.

Sneaking Up on the Problem – The intention here is to "distance" the client from going directly into an issue to minimize emotional pain. **Sneaking up is more a concept or strategy than a technique.**

Until the overall intensity is below six, focus on less intense issues or aspects *before* going to a painful event or trauma. Work with small bits of the situation or related parts that do not bring up strong emotions. Any technique that gives the client distance, any practice that does not go straight to the issue, that maintains some distance for the client and the emotional pain, is a Sneaking Up approach. This includes Constricted Breathing and focusing on body sensations. You can also use the concept of **sneaking away** to back off from an intense issue or to go more slowly and gently.

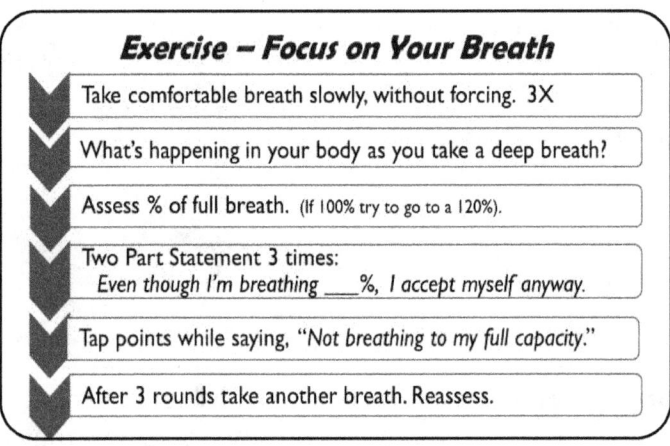

Constricted Breathing – We tend to take a more shallow breath when we are upset. Using EFT to address our current percentage of a full breath is a simple way to address our upset without having to think about "what to say." This is useful

- as a quick calming method
- as an exercise to introduce EFT,
- as a demonstration of EFT to a group,

- as a distancing tool if high intensity,
- when stuck or need a break
- to assign as "homework."

CHALLENGES

When EFT gets "stuck," or you are not sure where to go next, or you are not having the results you'd expect, some of the issues you could address are:

- Is the issue being addressed too globally?
- Is there a detail you've missed?

- Is there a conflict you have not yet identified?
- Have you tapped long enough?
- Is there an underlying issue that needs clearing first?
- Do you need to add more points?
- Do you need a stronger, more detailed Setup more closely related to the "real" feelings or issue?
- Try saying the Setup VERY LOUDLY.
- Is more detective work needed to discover what's interfering with the progress?

- Could there be additional issues, emotions surfacing, that need addressing now, before returning to the original focus to complete?

- Are you in your way? Working on your issues is important to stay impartial, to increase your awareness of your own biases and triggers.

- Is there too much intensity? Do you need to back up and focus on breathing, body sensations, and active listening?

- Are you asking irrelevant questions? Stick to pertinent investigative questions.

- Are you offering solutions? This tends to bring up resistance, the "yes, buts," and could negatively impact rapport. *It is not our role to give advice.*

- The client may be overloaded, not able to focus, and needs a break. Sessions can go only as fast as the most resistant part.

- Are you trying to do too much too soon for the client? Do they need more time to process?

- While rare, could there be an environmental issue interfering with your progress, such as food, beverages, the environment you are in, the chemicals present, etc.?

HELPFUL CONCEPTS

▶ **The Apex Effect** - The client cannot yet accept that EFT was responsible for the change. The client is unable to explain what has happened and will attribute it to something else they better understand. Keep records of issues worked on.

▶ **Hydration** – While there is no research as to the effect of being or not being hydrated on EFT results, most energy practitioners feel hydration is an important factor. Most offer water during sessions and encourage the client to have water available with online sessions.

▶ **Secondary Gain or Psychological Reversal** – *There is loss and there is gain with any change.* We don't like changes. We'd rather the situation or the other person change! Look for a possible gain from the behavior/sabotage, a benefit which the client has, or does not have, conscious awareness. Ask a variation of, what will you gain or lose by giving up the issue, behavior, or thing? Or what is the upside to keeping this problem? What is the downside of getting rid of it? Who or what might get in the way of resolving this?

▶ **The Personal Peace Procedure** – recommended practice to help guide self-care. Create a list of events in your life that are still bothersome and pick something from the list to address every day. Persistence is necessary for maximum benefit. *Self-care practice, like continuous learning, is a critical component of being an effective practitioner.* We will never be finished! We will never resolve every single issue or every single event we ever experienced. *What we gain is a great deal of awareness and emotional peace, increased calmness, and greater intuition, and better decision making.*

▶ **Calibration** – the practice of watching for minute changes in the client's behavior, movement, skin tone, facial expressions, breathing rates, voice tone, and inflections, how emotions are expressed. Calibrating is an essential part of successful EFT. Watch body language carefully. Never assume, always clarify meaning with the client.

▶ **Cognitive Shifts** – When the client decreases his or her intensity enough to be able to look at the situation more realistically, they typically come up with their own "reframe" or cognitive shift. When the intensity is below a three, often the client will spontaneously revise their perception on their own. *The goal for most counseling and coaching is to help the client develop a healthier perspective, a "cognitive* *shift."* Developing an individual and unique cognitive shift is powerful – and a delight to watch.

▶ **Working with Friends** – EFT sessions can shift the existing relationship. Be careful, set boundaries, and be respectful of the relationship dynamic. Again, never push EFT on anyone no matter how good a friend, no matter how much you may think it can help them. One option would be to tap without words. However, even tapping without words can bring up intense emotions they may not have been willing to share otherwise.

ADVANCED TOPICS COVERED IN MORE DEPTH IN LEVEL 3 CLASSES

The expectation for Level 2 is for the student to become proficient using Level 2 skills such as developing rapport, relevant Setups, detective work, using questions, and addressing aspects of an issue. Become effective in using basic skills before adding advanced techniques. While Level 2 *introduces the concepts of reframes, intuition, positive wording, and choices, these concepts are not* covered in depth until Level 3. This is a good reason to take a Level 3 class

Reframes – *If a client has not already developed a cognitive shift.* The timing, the type of reframe, and the intent are all critical components of successful reframes. Reframes are always *offered* by the practitioner and checked with the client for accuracy. Reframes can be misused, offered too early for the client to accept, used to influence a client, lead them down a different path, push the practitioner's agenda or ideas, or reflect the practitioner's judgments and biases. *Practitioner reframes are not the goal of a session.* **Reframing is not a necessary part of a successful resolution for the client.**

Children – Work first with the parent. Help the parent deal with his or her issues around the child's problem. This also allows you to learn more about family dynamics. As with adults, rapport is critical in gaining cooperation with children. While they often respond quickly with EFT, the challenge is gaining cooperation. Don't push.

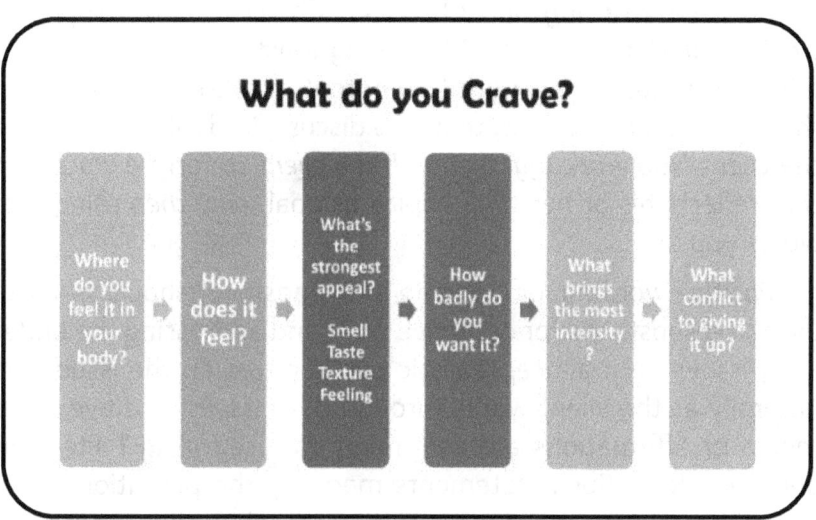

Addictive Behaviors – most often driven by anxiety and self-sabotaging limiting beliefs and early childhood traumatic events. Addictive behaviors always begin as an attempt at a solution. It is a coping mechanism, for an underlying problem they have not yet figured a way to resolve. Addiction is *not* the problem; it is their perceived solution to a problem. Teach EFT for relaxation and to address cravings. Explore any background of trauma, work on areas in which the client is exhibiting self-sabotage. While *working with serious addiction issues such as drug abuse or alcoholism requires additional training*, EFT often works successfully to address specific cravings.

Surrogate Tapping – The term is often used interchangeably with "Proxy Tapping." EFTi Glossary defines surrogate tapping as "tapping on behalf of another person, **animals**, or even a younger self, someone deceased or unconscious." Either way, someone is doing the tapping for, or instead of, another with the intent for someone else to "borrow benefits" from *your* tapping about *their* issue. Whether you are tapping as a replacement (surrogate) or a representative (proxy), make sure you first *clear your own emotions around the other's issue.* The only focus should be toward the outcome for *their* highest and best interest.

Positive Wording and Choices – Choices, as developed by Dr. Patricia Carrington, EFT Founding Master who died in 2019, differs from Reframes. With Carrington's method, you first work through strong emotions, then you discuss, in-depth, the goals of the client. You work *together with the client* to form a statement that reflects his or her clear choice or goal, *only then* using their words you tap.

Positive wording, or "tapping in the positive" should never be used as a substitute for detective work and addressing the underlying issues. In practice, realistic perspectives on the issue arise naturally as the client works through their issues. Positive statements or affirmations are commonly misused in EFT literature and on videos. Such statements made by the practitioner may "force" a positive concept on a client rather than allowing them to work through the issues allowing a different perspective to arise *from* the client. Using positive wording or choices should only be considered after significant progress on an issue and the intensity is below three. Neither positive wording nor choices are necessary for a successful resolution.

Know your Limits – With Level 2 skills there remains a need for mentoring and additional training to gain increased experience before engaging deeply with clients. **Maintain referral sources, find an experienced mentor, and practice regular tapping and self-care.**

ETHICAL ISSUES

- Your job as a practitioner is to create and hold a "safe space" for the client to share.

- The focus of the session should be on the client. Use the client's words. Check your wording with the client for their agreement. Never assume you know or that your perception/experience is the same. While you may begin globally, the goal is to find a specific detail/sensation focus for tapping.

- Always go at the pace of the client. They may not be "ready" to address their issue as quickly as you would prefer. "Resistance" to addressing deep issues is common. Never push *your* reframe.

- Address your issues – While we are never "done" in discovering issues to address with tapping, you will increase intuition and your effectiveness and ability to be fully present with your client, and decrease the chances that your issues and biases interfere with the session.

- The focus of all EFT sessions should be on the client's needs. Questions should be appropriate to the issue and not merely from your curiosity. Learn to live with not knowing.

- If someone presents with a physical problem, assure they have consulted their appropriate medical/physical professional.

- Set appropriate boundaries for your clients and respect their boundaries.

- Confidentiality is critical around any session, whether you are charging for a session or giving away a freebie. Information often comes out that generally would *not* be shared with others.

- Rapport is critical. The tone of voice should be calming, soothing.

- Introducing EFT – While it is good to have several "elevator" speeches that can briefly describe EFT, it is best to match your explanation with what can best be a bridge to their understanding and belief system.

POUND IT HOME POINTS

- The unifying concept for all techniques is to treat every individual as just that – an individual.
- Everyone makes their own interpretations as to the meaning of any situation.
- The EFT Process can be easy; people can be very complex.**
- Never assume anything about anyone. Assumptions can lead you down the wrong road.
- Stay curious. Check everything with the client.
- Everyone has their own path, their own journey, their own timing.**
- Everybody wants something. Help them discover what they want, and address what's in their way.
- Get to a Specific. Get details. Use investigative questions. Tap with their words, their key phrases, even in the Setup.
- Useful Default Questions: What comes up for you now? How do you know that?
- Never push forgiveness. Never push, period.
- Reframes can be an excuse for your agenda, use carefully if at all.
- There is almost always a conflict in changing. Find the loss and/or the gain.
- Resistance is normal. Accept it. Discover what is behind or underneath it.

BRIEFLY ABOUT HIGH INTENSITY

- Traumatic events, big and small, can happen to anyone. Fortunately, with support and time, many of us may resolve the impact of trauma. Unresolved traumatic events, however, can intrude into our present lives affecting our ability to cope, to "live, love and work," in a meaningful and satisfying way. In some cases, emotions can be so overwhelming the person tends to avoid places, people, and situations that could trigger the memory and the intense emotional reactions. Even "small" traumas can impact us because the decisions made at the time about ourselves, others, and the world continue to create challenges in some, if not all parts, of life and relationships.

- Go slowly, focus on less intense parts first.

- Working with people who have experienced *severe* trauma requires more experience and knowledge than is available in a Level 2 class. Create referral sources, seek out a mentor.

- Addressing a traumatic event could trigger an "**abreaction,**" defined by EFTi as a "normal but undesirable intense reaction to a trauma or trigger. These intense reactions are more likely to occur if the emotions connected to the traumatic event have long been repressed or buried."

- If the client does become very upset, or experiences abreaction, and is not able or willing to continue tapping, one option is to take the client's hand and tap their hand points, use reassuring statements, "You are here with me, You're safe now. It's ok, stay with me," etc. Ensure you have permission from the client, and that touching the client is within your licensing or governmental regulation. Because many sessions are online, it's helpful to have information about your client's living situation, a significant other's phone number, and some history as to their past mental health and trauma history. It is even more important online to work gradually toward painful issues and keep the client in the present time. If necessary, "break state." (See below.)

- *Some intensity is expected, perhaps necessary, however practitioners attempt to prevent abreactions.* Carefully calibrate, and listen to your client. Modify your approach based on their reaction. *Be ready to back up, slow down, change procedure.*

- Abreactions in the mental health world are defined more seriously as a very highly emotional reaction to *reliving* the event. They seem to be "back there." The strength of their reaction can seem "over-the-top" and disconcerting to a new practitioner—a good reason to always tap *with* your client to keep yourself calm.

- You do not want your client to react as if the trauma were recurring. Work to keep the client in the present moment. Stay with current body sensations, with what they are feeling *now*.

- Intense reactions can come unexpectedly. EFT's tools are designed to go slowly, gently, gradually into an event.

> **Sometimes the fastest way to "get there" is to slow down.****

- Help the client to gain awareness.
- Tap for their level of breathing and existing body sensations.
- Tap using a distancing tool, e.g., a container.
- *When their upset does not calm quickly, it may be best to "break state" by giving grounding instructions such as, look at me, where are you, feel your butt in the chair,*

what color is the carpet, let's stop and get some water, etc. When calm, focus on the breath or use another distancing technique.

- The possibility of abreaction is one of the reasons practitioners work to develop a strong rapport and level of trust with the client. Use lots of empathic statements.

- Listen. Watch. Calibrate. Pay close attention to any changes in emotions or body language, e.g., body and eye movements, breathing rate, tone of voice, skin tone, etc. and modify your approach to minimize upset.

- Check frequently by asking such questions as, "What's going on with you now?" Or "What comes up for you now?" Or "What just happened?" Their answers help guide you as they shift aspects, i.e., move to a different aspect, the emotion has changed or move to another memory.

- *Develop a consistent self-practice of EFT to maintain your composure and decrease incidents of being triggered by a client's emotion.*

- **Assure your client leaves in a calm state.**

EFT IS SIMPLE—PEOPLE ARE COMPLEX

Download a copy of the EFT Flow Chart from https://www.AnnAdams.com/FlowChart

Or a copy of this review https://www.AnnAdams.com/EFTReview

Find More Resources such as books often recommended by trainers and other helpful tools at

https://www.AnnAdams.com/Resources

FREE RESOURCES:

~Introductory Tapping Manual by EFT International at EFT International.org

~Introduction to EFT – A beginner's guide for approaching individual problems at Ann Adams.com/IntroEFT

~Gary Craig EFT Tutorial – https://emofree.com/english/eft-tapping-tutorial-en.html

NOTES

CREDITS: * EFT International Glossary or Google EFT International glossary:

** An Annism

Slides are from EFT4PowerPoint Training Package - Version 3020 or were created specifically for this handout. More about the workshop in a box, go to https://www.EFT4PowerPoint.com

ADDITIONAL OPTIONS FOR TAPPING

The basic formula for EFT works – as it is! There are multiple variations on EFT and additional ways to approach client issues, some useful, some not so much – each has their proponents and their critics. Like our clients, each practitioner is an individual. An approach that fits well with you and your client population may not work at all for another. Fortunately, you do not have to be knowledgeable or skillful with the many variations and optional ways of addressing the client's issues to experience results. You do not have to become an expert in every variation. The basic formula for EFT works – as it is!

As part of an EFT training, however, trainers may mention or introduce a variety of additional options for tapping and addressing client issues. It would not be possible for every option, advanced technique, and other skillful "Art of Delivery" to be taught in the time frames for the Level 1 and 2 classes. Here are some of the options a trainer may mention during the basic EFT classes. Continuing learning from both reading and attending advanced training is encouraged.

EFT IS SIMPLE—PEOPLE ARE COMPLEX

The below are common minor modifications on EFT.

Head Point – The head point was added to the EFT tapping points after a demonstration in Gary Craig's video set, Beyond the Basics, by Michael Gandy, an acupuncturist. Gandy demonstrated the **head** point—located on top of the head between the ears, and the wrist and ankle points.

Wrist Point and Ankle Points – The other two points, along with the Head point, were recommended by Gandy as a substitute for the original EFT formula with 14 EFT points. Tap both sides of the wrist and ankle. The **wrist** point is located about two fingers above the wrist crease. The **ankle** point is four inches above the protruding bone. NOTE: The **ankle point** is contraindicated for use with pregnant women as it *may* be possible to trigger contractions or cause early termination.

Finger Points and Back of the Hand – In the original EFT formula, the finger points were tapped in the corner of the fingernail on the body side of the nail with the palm facing down. This included tapping on the thumb, index, middle and little fingernails. The ring finger was skipped as that meridian was covered when using the 9 Gamut exercise (described below.) If the fingers *are* used, without the 9 Gamut, practitioners often tap all the fingers.

ADDITIONAL OPTIONS FOR TAPPING

Some practitioners tap both sides of the fingernails in a "pinching" like motion.

The Liver Point – Used in TFT and was part of the original EFT points. This point is located about an inch below the nipple. Since this point is a bit awkward for women, it was often skipped or a point lower on the liver meridian was used. However, some practitioners still consider the Liver meridian important and substitute another acupuncture point further down the Liver meridian at the end of the first floating rib. Rather than find the exact spot on the liver meridian, the student/client can place the heel of their hands on the last ribs and pat with the entire hand.

More About Points – None of the above, now optional, meridian points listed above are listed in Gold Standard EFT. Unlike TFT, it is not necessary to "diagnose" which points are needed in what order; the order of the points does not matter for success in EFT. Which points you use on a meridian may not matter either as several individual practitioners have shown that points lower or higher on a meridian can be substituted successfully and Michael Gandy's 3 points are effective. However, for ease of use and consistency of training and definition of EFT, EFT trainers should use the EFT points as taught, SOH, head, nose side of eyebrow, boney side of the eye, bone under eye, under nose, under lower lip, "collarbone," and underarm, as they run down the body. Experiment only after you become skilled at the successful use of EFT on a variety of people and issues.

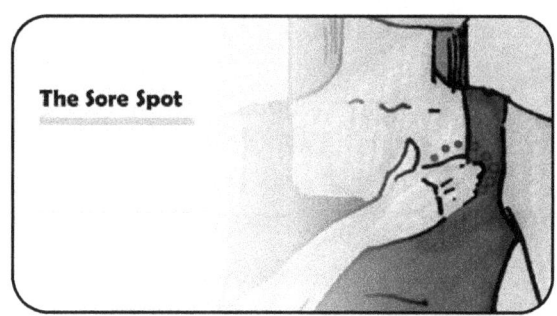

The Sore Spot

Sore Spots – are located on both sides of the chest. Neurolymphatic reflex points, discovered in 1930 by an osteopath, Dr.

Frank Chapman, these points are located around the body and assist with lymphatic drainage and have several health benefits. In TFT and EFT, the "sore spot" was initially used as a substitute for the side of the hand point as a means of counteracting psychological reversal. Craig dropped its use as it was more time consuming and harder to teach.

The 9 Gamut Exercise – Tap the slight indentation about one inch up from the V shape between the ring and little finger on the back of the hand towards the wrist. Some practitioners add the back of the hand point as an extra point in the tapping sequence. The 9 Gamut exercise is useful when

EFT seems slow or stuck

The session seems to be "heavy"

You've cleared a lot and want to reinforce the learning or

It just "seems" to be a good idea.

While tapping continuously on the back of the hand, hold your head level and steady through all the steps. Close your eyes, Open your eyes, look hard down to the right, then hard down left, roll your eyes around the periphery of your vision as if you were a grandfather clock, hum a few musical bars, count to 7, hum a few musical bars again. The musical bar can be any tune or made up.

ADDITIONAL TAPPING STRATEGIES

Floor to Ceiling Eye Roll – Introduced by Roger Callahan's TFT, this exercise is useful when intensity is down to 1 or 2. Holding your head level, tap continuously on the gamut point as you move your eyes to the floor. Then *slowly roll your eyes up* as far as they will go, *and back down, while still tapping*. While it is no longer mandated to teach by EFTi, the Eyeroll can be helpful when the intensity is low.

Touch and Breathe – Instead of tapping the points, touch each as you take a slow breath while tuning into your issue.

Talk and Tap (or Rant) – Tap as you are telling the story without interruption.

ADDITIONAL OPTIONS FOR TAPPING

Continual Tapping – as above but also can mean to tap continually throughout the day, e.g., on the finger points.

Additional Options for Sneaking Up – As an addition to the Movie Technique, have the client run the movie, using the NLP technique the Fast Phobia Cure, and imagining going into a theater, find a seat, or go first into the projection booth. You can run the movie in slow motion, fast forward, backward, create cartoon characters for each character, use an imaginary remote to control the speeds, put images far away, run it in black and white. Options are limited only by your imagination and the client's response.

Using a Container – Additional gentle distancing techniques include having the client put the issue in a self-described **container**, then tap for descriptions of the container, or for what is in it, or for that "thing on the other side of the ocean." Imagining the problem in a container can also be a way of offering effective *closure or "containing"* any remaining intensity toward the end of a session.

Sneaking Up on the Problem
Strong Emotions not Necessary

- Circle around issue to prevent FEAR of addressing event.
- Focus on body sensations, use code name, no details.
- Create general Setups about fear and physical response.
- Repeat until 3 or below.
- Only then address details.
- Start with a "tiny piece".

APPENDIX 2

In Pursuit of Excellence

In Pursuit of Excellence

> Note: This article summarizes important aspects of using EFT I have spoken about many times, and includes points from the article I wrote for *EFT and Beyond,* an informative and useful book for all practitioners. There is also a DVD discussing these issues informally.
> https://www.AnnAdams.com/store

Our goal as practitioners is to gain excellence in delivering EFT and excellence in all aspects of our practice. Experience is essential, but experience alone does not create excellence. It is possible to have experience without growth, to have practice without learning, to work without wisdom. The pursuit of excellence is about increasing mastery of ourselves through the pursuit of inner knowledge. Excellence is found in ongoing learning and growth. As those of you familiar with the Abraham-Hicks tapes know they tell us that, "We never get it all done."

In my talk for Gary Craig's EFT DVD Specialty Series 1 on Working with Severely Disturbed Children, I discussed intrinsically connected characteristics that contribute to developing excellence:

1. Get yourself out of the way. We are facilitators; the client is the healer.

2. Be congruent—or as the kids say, "walk your talk."
3. Be unattached to the outcome—respect the client has the needed resources within.
4. Stay in the here and now—be present with your client.
5. Stand out from the long line of other "helpers"—use creativity when needed in the art of delivery.
6. Respect our clients—admire their courage and their ability to heal themselves.
7. Be a Professional—with a capital P in all we do.

Those seven characteristics remain true whether working with children or adults.

FIRST: Get yourself out of the way

Mastery of anything includes mastery of yourself. Getting yourself out of the way is a whole lot easier if there is <u>less</u> of you to get out of the way! For true excellence in our practice, we need to have cleared the major traumas and limiting beliefs in our lives. We never resolve 100% of the issues impacting our life. What we gain is increased awareness of our triggers, the pitfalls, the limitations. You gain a life with less defensiveness, anxiety, and anger. You create confidence that shines through in everything you do.

You have come to believe that everyone is doing the best they can, **including yourself.** And, if it is any comfort, we all still have work to do. We all make what we consider mistakes. But take heart, treat yourself gently. As Abraham says, "We can't get it wrong, because we will never get it ALL done." We will always continue to be a *work in progress.*

SECOND: Be congruent

What you say that you believe guides what you do and is reflected in how you manage your sessions, how you conduct your practice, how you live your life, what you choose as marketing material. Each piece congruently reflects the other. You are clear on the all-important concept—Whose problem is whose?

There is an old Charlie Brown cartoon in which Snoopy is talking to his bird friend, "We (dogs) are the highest form of life on this earth! The world revolves around us!" The next panel shows a concerned Snoopy asking, "Doesn't it?" We, like Snoopy, are all a bit egocentric. We all try in some way to define the world as revolving around us. And we, like Snoopy, also realize with anxiety and concern that we are *not* the center of the world.

Some of you will deny this. You will say, "Oh, no, that's not me. I don't think the world is, or should be, revolving around me. I am always thinking of others." Then, consider the below quote for those of you who deny your ego and believe you always put others first:

> **"People who are always thinking of the feelings of others can be very destructive because they are hiding so much from themselves."**
> **- May Sarton**

The congruent person understands and accepts that each of us defines our world and colors our world through our individual perceptions and experiences. This awareness leads to understanding and compassion for the way others color their world.

The congruent practitioner fully understands boundaries. It is easy for them to say, "I don't understand. Can you explain what you mean?" Or "Don't think that worked. Let's back up and try that again." Or "I don't agree with that. Is there common ground that we can find?" Or "I am not willing to do that."

What helps the congruent practitioner on the road to excellence is a clear set of *beliefs and boundaries*. They can *set limits* for themselves and others in a calm but truthful and respectful way. They are certainly not perfect, but they understand the importance of *self-care, self-acceptance, and self-awareness*, goals we all work toward as we clear our "stuff."

THIRD: Join NATO - <u>N</u>ot <u>A</u>ttached <u>T</u>o The <u>O</u>utcome

Being unattached to the outcome comes from *fully* respecting that the client has *within themselves the ability to heal themselves.* You realize you are merely a tool in their journey. We don't heal anyone; EFT does not heal anyone or any medical issue. We and EFT are facilitators; the client is the healer.

Being unattached doesn't mean we don't care. We continue to look for ways to get through to each client. Any part we play in the client's healing comes, as Gary Craig said, *through* us, not *by* us. Accepting this concept is the forerunner, maybe even the foundation, of allowing our intuition to develop. It can take a while to realize that *all healing comes from within our clients,* and any effective facilitating comes *through* us, not *by* us.

After giving the talk on working with children, I received emails like, "How do I "*get*" my child (or niece or grandchild, etc.) to "*do EFT*"? Look at that closely. How do I *get* them to do it? How do you feel when someone is trying to *get* you to do something? Do you feel they have your best interest at heart or more likely do you feel they have their agenda they are attempting to impose? Trying to *get* someone to do anything means you are attached to the outcome. You are pushing your agenda.

FOURTH: Stay in here and now

Being totally present, in the present, is easier said than done, but is critical for developing your intuition, for allowing the work to be *through* you. When you are in the here and now, you are attuning to and trusting the process, that is occurring between the two of you in the room together. *Right now, right here, right in this moment.*

Staying in the here and now means there is no "then," there is just "now." You are without judgment. Judgment needs history to operate.

One of the attractions of EFT is that it is so quick and often so effective that we can forget that part of what works is the process of the relationship. What happens in the therapy room, right now, between two people is full of meaning. Meaning that is important to the process and outcome of a session.

So, before we rush to intervene and start thinking about the best Setup, or the next investigative question, we need to take a deep breath and attend closely to less conscious factors. Healing often takes place in tiny moments and small places in a relationship. *Pay attention to what is happening in the moment,* a process that may be lost in our need to make therapy as brief and problem-focused as possible. It can be lost in your effort and your need to "do" something to help. We may feel pressure to show how skilled and smart and knowledgeable or even how intuitive we are. We want so much to be helpful.

> **Being helpful is not always helpful.**

Before we consider "doing something," remember there is meaning everywhere, in every action: when we are patient, when we honor their timing and their agenda, when we are willing to sit a while longer with our uncertainty and discomfort, and puzzlement.

We may tend to *jump right in*. After all, our intuition has already gone to where we need to go. Or has it? I have watched many a therapist barrel down a road of their supposed intuition. How do you know what is *your intuition versus your intervention?* NATO – No attachment to the outcome.

The problem is, we cannot always tell the difference between our agenda and our intuition. Intuition may generate excitement at first thought, but it quickly turns to a calm neutral feeling.

My thoughts on intuition:

- If you are feeling *sure* that this is what your client *needs* to do—it is probably *not* intuition.
- If you are all excited about it and you just can't wait to share your brilliant insight—it is probably *not* intuition.

- If you are attached to the outcome—it is *not* intuition.
- If you are pushing your agenda, attempting to convince the client—it is *not* intuition.

We are much better at *doing* than *being*.

Sally sat in our session, sketching on a pad. I started to get a bit antsy that maybe I was wasting our limited time together. I gently asked if there were some goals she'd like to work on or any issues she'd like to resolve. Sally gave me this pained look as only adolescents can. "Ms. Ann," she said, "Being with you here is the **only** place I have where I can just be me. Do we need to fix that?" Gulp. "You're right Sally," I said. "Just being is the most important thing."

Sometimes it is not about doing therapy or doing tapping or "doing" at all. It is about just being there fully present. And *sometimes, that is harder than providing a particular intervention.* Being with someone who is fully present and accepting where you are right now is can be what the client needs most to feel safe to take the next step. It is a gift they are not often given.

The desire to *do something* is your agenda. Helping the client to feel safe and ready is still a critical part of EFT. I have heard many therapists explain the reason that a client dropped out didn't make progress was that the client didn't want to change or wasn't ready to change. In a way, we are all resistant. After all, all changes are scary, even good changes. It is our job to help the client feel safe enough to begin to share their shame, guilt, and deepest fears of inadequacy.

We are responsible *to* our client but not *for* our client.

With EFT as an important tool, the progress can move even faster after they feel they can be who they are. It is true, despite our very best efforts our client gets no progress or leaves too soon, no one can be all things to all people. There is that occasional person who is not yet ready despite our best efforts to create rapport and *provide a safe place to be who they are.* Develop the ability to fully, deeply listen, and attune to your client. Listening is still the most important key to getting through to a client. Being fully and deeply heard is a basic human need.

EFT is an incredible tool. It works amazingly quickly on those nice, clean, specific situations. However, the client is not always specific in their presenting problem. They come in because their life is not going well for them. It takes a lot of that detective work to find the underlying issue. Less experienced practitioners stay general. The seasoned practitioner knows how to guide a general issue into the specifics behind it.

A strong bond is formed when you ask careful questions and listen *carefully* to the answer. The participant feels you care what he or she thinks and feels. And being heard and understood is a basic human social need.

Detective work is more than asking investigative questions or deep, thought-provoking questions. The level of rapport and timing for a question are critical factors as well. Questions are a link to what is locked up in our psyche. In another Charlie Brown cartoon, Lucy is asking Linus, "How can holding a blanket make you feel secure?" The following scenes show his face vividly as he struggles with his internal answer to that question. The question shakes up his world.

Professional coaches and top-notch managers and supervisors have long understood the power of questions. Amateurs look for instant results. The professional realizes that *unless the answer comes from within, it has little or no meaning for the person. Worse, there is no ownership of the solution.*

FIFTH: Setting yourself apart—be creative and flexible

It is helpful to set yourself apart from the long line of others who have said, "I'm here to help you." Many of our clients are with us as almost a last chance for a solution. Some EFT Practitioners either feel that EFT is the *only* thing to use or worse, EFT is the only tool they have. Gary Craig was often creative in dealing with clients. Creativity added to the EFT techniques is often necessary to go past client defenses.

At an EFT Masters Retreat, my role was to ensure it all ran smoothly and take care of problems. A participant approached me saying she'd come as a last resort, that nothing she'd done for years had helped. Worse, she said she didn't feel this workshop was helping either and that she'd wasted her time and money. She sounded very depressed but, in a way, almost proud.

We become very attached to our "stuff."

Much truth to the quote, "Despair itself, if it goes on long enough, can become a kind of sanctuary in which one settles down and feels at ease." So many long-term clients identify with their issues to the degree that they don't see who they would be without them. It is challenging to work through all their fears and defenses and reversals.

The participant had been working with highly qualified, skilled EFT practitioners. Hmm. What to do? I had an inspiration. I gave the preframe, "Game to do something totally different?" She looked puzzled but agreed. I asked her to take all her problems and place them on the ground beside us. Then, to describe how all those problems looked to her now. This was a disconcerting question for someone prone to intellectualizing. She was taken out of her head; it shook up her world. She had a blank look and said, "I have never done this before." I replied, "That's the point, you said what you'd been doing wasn't working."

She described the problems as a huge, ugly, green chalkboard. On it was written in large thick writing, in multiple layers, and different colors, all the negative things in her life. What color and how big and how thick? She used her hands to describe it. I didn't ask for an intensity rating, another difference. My "test" of whether we would be successful was if one of the writings got lighter or disappeared. Focusing on one statement and one layer at the time, we tapped. After each round, I instructed, "Pretend you have an eraser in your hand and erase that layer of words from your board."

> **Metaphors are useful and physical movements can offer a totally different perspective on a problem.**

After she'd erased the statement, we'd addressed the next one until she reported that everything written on her board was wiped clean. It took a while. "Awesome," I said. We took a few seconds to celebrate the change. I then asked what she'd like written instead. She formulated new statements that were both respectful and positive. I asked her to use her hand to write each new sentence on the board as I tapped on her. She started with, "I am worthy."

My job at the retreat was to help a person feel safe enough to take the next step so they could go back to their group and participate fully. So, after filling the board with the positive statements she would prefer to read on her board, we addressed her fear that EFT was not working for her, that she was too messed up for it to work, and that she was wasting her time and money following a pipe dream.

She went back to the group. The rest of the retreat went well for her. She worked on many issues with her family and others who had put those negative writings on her walls—or in her case, her chalkboard.

What was a bit different or creative about the session was the separation of the person from her tightly held issues through metaphor and using the physical movement of her body in physically erasing and writing on the board. What was very much the same is that I listened carefully to her concerns. I had no agenda. She was operating totally in her head, as we therapists say, and she was conflicted. How could she resolving anything; her identity was tied to that green chalkboard. My intuition was to separate her from her issues, to get "out of her head." How did the idea occur to me? I have no clue. It was just there. Did we solve all her long-term problems? Of course not. But we shifted her perspective sufficiently for her to begin baby steps toward changing her view of herself and her world.

Where does "intuition" come from? There are many theories. But from wherever it travels I am convinced that easy access to intuition is the result of getting yourself out of the way, working on whatever your issues to gain awareness and ability to self-regulate your emotions.

Anyone can go through an EFT sequence. I taught EFT to a four-year-old and watched as she ran her doll through a great EFT sequence. So cute, tapping on her baby doll with, "Even though you are feeling sad, you are a really good dolly, and I love you." Tap, tap, tap. Delightful! And, easy. A four-year-old can learn and apply effective EFT. With the effectiveness of EFT, sometimes that's all it takes.

One of my own favorite EFT cousins is Touch and Breathe. Touch and Breathe uses the EFT points but with a gentle touch paired with a slow deep breath instead of the usual tapping. Some people like a slower more gentle approach than tapping.

For instance, a woman who bought the EFT4 PowerPoint Comprehensive EFT Training Package traveled to help Tsunami survivors. She emailed after she returned saying the residents didn't like tapping. It had scared these people because it was "like the waves coming." It can be helpful to be creative and to have a few other approaches for those complex situations where you need a bit of creativity to get over a hump.

Listening, fully listening, to our clients can be challenging. You are listening with both ears, both eyes, your heart, and your entire body are all focused on this client at this moment. You may have ideas about what is happening, certainly, but you have no preset agenda. If you are truly not attached to the outcome, if you have truly gotten yourself out of the way, you can see and hear your client fully. It just flows.

We develop intuition by having a clear enough inner world to hear that inner voice, that inner guidance. We quiet our chatter within to hear it. It is a total focus on the client. A total being in the here and now or *being in the zone* as professionals in many fields call it.

I cannot stress enough to develop excellence in EFT is to do your work.

SIXTH: Respect for the client's ability to heal

Another factor for true excellence is the respect you have for the client's ability to resolve their problem. Anything less devalues and disempowers our clients.

This is a soapbox I frequent. I pound the drum for respecting the client's ability to resolve his or her problem. My definition of respect is tied to the belief that we are all born with an innate ability to heal. This includes:

- Everything that the person needs is within.

- We do not solve the problem, heal anyone, or fix anything; we share our tools.

- We do not tell them what they *should* do. We do not *"should"* on our clients. We are guides and resources. We help them access their inner strength.

- We admire their courage. Some have had such severe traumas that it seems amazing that they get up in the morning to face another day. I am in awe of the resilience of people. Respect their resilience and courage.

- We may teach skills and alternatives, but only when necessary, and always in the form of an educational suggestion or, even better, as a question.

- We come into this world with all we need. We spend our lives learning to access it. Our job is to guide our clients through the process. Not to lead them down *our* healing road.

We are often very tempted to give advice or tell someone what they should do or share our brilliant ideas for alternatives. That's not our job. Our job is to help them access their inner resources. Occasionally we share an alternative, give a suggestion; I am not even opposed to occasional advice. Remember the power of questions. To be meaningful, the answer must come from within.

All of us have given a suggestion or advice to a client and had it fall flat. Or the client agrees that it was a good idea, but they don't follow it. Why does our advice fail? Because advice is all about us. It is not about them. It did not come from the client.

> **Giving advice is a doubtful remedy but generally not dangerous—since it has so little effect.**
> **- Jung**

In my years as a social worker, I have given terrific advice. The client agreed it was the perfect solution. Did they then follow up and do it? Rarely. We've all given advice. It seems to be a universal way we attempt to help one another. It is just not very effective.

> **The urge to give advice is human.**
> **The ability to ignore advice is even MORE human.**

Even when the client pays for advice, whether it be from a physician or financial planner, do they always follow their advice? No. WHY? They have not dealt with their internal conflicts about the issue. Our job is to create a safe haven and guide them through conflicts and feelings and limiting beliefs.

However, I have watched practitioners give more than educational suggestions. I have watched as the practitioner told the client what they think the client *should* be doing. All in the name of their supposed *intuition*. Again, we do not "*should*" on our clients. We do not lead our clients down *our* road. A key stumbling block for newbies is what I call "leading" or having an agenda that you then impose on your client. I am using the word leading like the judge who tells the attorney to stop leading the witness. Leading, in the way I am using the term, is the opposite of being a member of NATO.

When you are leading the client, you are *very* attached to the outcome. That's the problem.

Reframing is a marvelous EFT skill, and investigative questions used in detective work can be powerful. But reframing and questions can also be disguised as leading or pushing your agenda on your client.

While there are exceptions, for the most part, our clients want to please us. Because of this tendency, when we use our agenda and start tapping for how he or she *should* feel, what he *should* think, or what he *should* do then they tend to go along. Even when we tell our clients, "I want you to interrupt me and change the words and set me "straight" many still will not correct the practitioner.

In one session, I watched the practitioner asked a disguised leading question, "Don't you want to feel better about yourself by doing these exercises?" The client responded, "If I don't agree, I wouldn't be giving *you* what *you* want."

That is a rare client. A true professional in that situation would have identified their error and gone, "Ulph," then regrouped to go another direction. Unfortunately, the practitioner in this instance was so *into* her direction, so sure she knew what would be best, she continued down that road and lost rapport with the client who sat there patiently to the end. The practitioner lost the client. He followed up with another EFT practitioner. Clients tend to vote with their feet.

Clients rarely contradict a therapist who is head over tails into his or her agenda. A client needs to be sure you are doing your best to fully hear and understand before they feel safe to contradict you. One danger from having your agenda is that you are not listening, and the client does not feel safe to go deeply into his or her issues. And, sometimes feeling safe takes a while. Safety equates to trust, and trust takes time to grow.

If you are taking a client down *your road* or even their road but at *your speed* and they may be unable to give you what they believe *you* want. He couldn't meet your expectation gets in the way of the client's healing. You have added more guilt and more disappointment in themselves. One more time the client feels inadequate; they failed one more time to live up to someone else's expectation.

A practitioner once asked why his clients often waited until their hand was on the doorknob at the end of the sessions to bring up an important issue. Partly, this has to do with a client's safety issues, which take time to identify and resolve, time to build that trust. As the practitioner told me about the session, it was clear he practitioner was leading and was following his agenda for the session. I asked the practitioner if he considered asking the client, after each round of tapping, *"What comes up for you now?"* "Oh!" he said, after a short pause.

When you reframe a client's statement or use your intuition, check it out with your client. *Every. Single. Time.* Feeling safe to contradict you takes more than a casual comment on the first session that they should interrupt you if you are wrong. *"What comes up for you now?"* is non-directive. It helps assures them there is no right or wrong answer. Every answer, every response, is feedback.

> **Leading is the opposite of respecting your client's ability to heal.**

I was supervising a class practice session when the identified client said, "It hurts so much that I just want to shut down and stop feeling anything." A great door to explore. The client's comment to stop feeling anything triggered something in the EFTer. She created the Setup, "Even though I want to shut down and not feel, I know I won't really shut down, feelings are important."

A reframe? No way. This was manipulation disguised as a reframe. This is a classic example of what I mean by leading or imposing our agenda. Leading a client stops rapport, stops a client from feeling safe to reveal the next deeper level.

The practitioner was pushing her agenda; she was attached to the outcome. She wanted to "save" her client. The result of pushing your agenda is that you've lost respect for your client's ability to resolve his or her problem. They feel it—it devalues their experience; it devalues their sense of self.

This newbie practitioner was triggered; she immediately was fearful for the client and wanted to "save" her.

I stopped the new EFTer and gently said that by using that Setup, she was imposing her belief instead of going where her client led. "After all," I said, "wanting to shut down is a very logical, rational thought when there is so much emotional pain. Who in their right mind wants to feel bad? Shutting down looks like a great option if you have no other tool." Our job as therapist is to share other options—like EFT. It is not our job to impose our agenda or values or our "shoulds" or "should nots."

Was this woman *actually* going to shut off her feelings? Well, she hadn't in the 20 years she'd had the problem. The client came up to me later and thanked me for intervening. "That was right on," she said, "I wasn't feeling heard. I was being taken where I didn't want to go." Keep in mind that she told me about her discomfort, not the practitioner. They won't always tell you.

Don't be afraid to follow where your client *is*, their deepest desire is to be heard and understood. Indeed, anything less than feeling heard understood, and accepted limits any therapy - even EFT. Our job is to be fully present with our clients while they work through their problems. When the issue is resolved the client looks at it differently.

NOTE: The only exception to the above would be when the client is a danger to themselves and others.

Clear the emotions. Cognitive shifts will follow.

We share the tools. The client discovers the cognitive shifts. The biggest thrill to me in using EFT is watching a client develop a cognitive shift. It is beautiful. The logic and realizations and even forgiveness happen naturally after resolving the issues. I feel gratitude at being there, being a part of a powerful force at work. We don't need to push it! And, we sure don't need to try to talk them out of feeling how they feel—as if we could anyway.

Many of my private clients are professionals who manage offices and supervise people. Since I have many years in managing and supervising people in a variety of settings, occasionally I do offer suggestions. However, until your client has resolved the personal issues that are triggered in the work environment and by his or her responsibilities, even the very best of solutions fall on deaf ears. I am not opposed to giving educational suggestions or even the occasional piece of advice. It is just rare that it is needed. And even rarer that the advice is followed.

Questions are *much* more powerful than advice or suggestions. Questions help us integrate information and learn, and process our experience differently. Ask yourself, before yielding to the temptation of giving advice, "Is this information the client doesn't have?" *"What need am I filling within myself in giving this advice?"*

> **We are so happy to advise others that we occasionally we even do it in their interest.**
> **- Jules Renard**

Teenagers often tune you out when you kick into the adult "lecture" mode. They see it as criticism. All they hear is, "Waaaa, Waaaa, Waaaa, Waaaa, Waaaa, Waaaa."

I mentored a teenager with many problems. Her older sister is her only family contact. This sister had her first baby and Tassy was very afraid that this baby would take her place and her sister would forget about her. She was upset, angry, and wanted to confront her sister. Staff at the group home had been making suggestions as to what she should do and were trying to convince her that her sister would still love her. It was not working.

I drove her to see her sister. As we had done many times before, we tapped on the hour and a half drive—no advice, no logic. This is a kid who had lost contact with everyone else in her family—they *had*, in effect, forgotten her. This was a logical fear for her. We tapped about all her feelings and fears. She was able to visit the sister and enjoy the baby. She changed her perception of the event from seeing it as a loss and being very fearful, to see the opportunity that she now had to be an aunt, to play a role in a larger family circle.

Remember the client who said, "I felt I was being taken where I wasn't ready to go." Timing issues are another stumbling block for practitioners. Trust the process. There was a book in the 60s called *Don't Push the River (It Flows by Itself)*. Guide a person skillfully, respectfully, through an EFT session, and their cognitive shifts happen naturally. Watching the person shift in their perception of the situation is the real magic of this work.

We use poor timing when we:

- Jump to a Setup we *think* they need without clarification from the client.

(Always clarify Setup wording before proceeding.)

- Attempt to address the positive *before* we deal with negative specific events.

(Clear the intensity around the event *first*.)

- Jumping ahead without working through the emotions.

(Narrow the issue to a specific event, time, place, thing, or person and work conscientiously to clear each the intensity with each aspect.)

- Go straight to forgiveness before they have exhausted their emotions about the issue.

(Wait for the client to bring up forgiveness.)

A client may not be ready to forgive for many sessions and introducing forgiveness can create resistance. Forgiveness may come later—or never. Never push.

The concept of forgiveness has many different meanings. My definition is that I have no further emotional involvement or investment in what that person did or said. I've let the emotions go. Isn't that what EFT does naturally? I question the need to introduce forgiveness at all. As a client removes all the negative emotions and the event is neutral for him or her there is a sense of peace, understanding, and acceptance that comes up naturally. Pushing forgiveness may stop their movement toward that awareness, acceptance, and understanding.

Therapy is still a process.

We are so eager to help that we sometimes forget that therapy, even therapy with EFT, is a process and that relationships and rapport are still important factors in resolving life's issues. Yes, we can resolve someone's long term issue and not have a rapport or a relationship, or even *like them*. But it is the exception, even in EFT.

When I first learned EFT in my newbie enthusiasm, I tried it on everyone. If you came within five feet of me, I had you tapping! My friends teased that no one was exempt. I have since learned much more discretion. Did I resolve specific issues? Yes. Did I reduce some of the pain? Sure. And, I had no relationship to speak of with these people.

EFT works so well and so often that newbies rush in where experienced people have learned caution. And, the newbies get results. The results of EFT often hide the inexperience or lack of knowledge of the practitioner. The amazing results of EFT lull the inexperienced, less educated practitioner into a false sense of competence. They begin thinking this is easy. Just tap and you solve everyone's problems. It takes a few times of stubbing your toe on complexities and losing a few clients to gain wisdom.

I get emails from newbies, *I just learned about EFT. It is fantastic! I always have success. How do I become an EFT Master?* I smile. I take a deep breath. I remember they are doing the best they can, and I send them a form letter. Developing mastery is **not** a quick process.

The problem with the apparent ease of EFT is that it may make you complacent. *I don't need to study or take a class. I know how to do this. You can learn it in five minutes. Just tap.* The importance of practice and the process of the relationship and the study of the nuances can be lost in the apparent ease of it all.

You become an excellent EFT practitioner through study and practice and practice and practice. When have stubbed toes many times. You realize that true excellence is acquired over time.

Most often EFT does make a person feel better if they just tap for a few minutes. It is, after all, a terrific calming technique, that doesn't necessarily depend on the skill of the practitioner. One theory behind how EFT and other energy techniques work is that when we stimulate the acupressure points, we are releasing feel-good chemicals into our bodies. We often feel better just tapping.

Well, sometimes.

"Julie" had been using EFT only a few months when she was challenged by a leader in her community to work on his wife to lose weight. Julie saw this as an opportunity to spread the EFT in her community. The man said he would pay her only if his wife lost weight. Julie had never worked with someone with a complex eating problem. She attacked it as a simple phobia. Unsurprisingly, the woman had many complex reasons for her weight, hidden motivations around the relationship with her husband, and many safety fears around losing weight. After six sessions the client reported feeling "worse" and had gained more weight. Julie bombed badly.

In retrospect and with wisdom Julie saw she made several mistakes, all of which tie into what we are talking about here. She was *attached to the outcome* she wanted to impress the community leader. She had *not gotten out of her way.* She was thinking of the opportunities she would; she was *not fully present for the client.* She *did not respect* the client; she was out to "prove" EFT worked. She was focusing on the husband's goals, not what the wife wanted or needed.

Problems are often complex.

Don't go where you don't belong. Get to know your client. Get lots of practice. Swap sessions with other EFTers. Train with someone who has lots of experience with EFT and has developed a successful practice. Getting consultation and mentoring and feedback from experienced practitioners.

We can become very attached to our problems.

But do we always have to have rapport and relationships? Well, no. Here's another story, I had a picnic for some friends on my patio and one friend brought a guest who had a fear of spiders. And, along came a little spider to the picnic. The guest reacted predictably hysterically. My friends, knowing I was studying EFT, challenged me to "fix" her. So, I did.

EFT IS SIMPLE—PEOPLE ARE COMPLEX

No preframe, no preamble, no questions about history, no real attempt at rapport, I didn't even ask her if she wanted to get over the fear of spiders. Everyone is standing there looking at me. In the impulsive spur of the moment that can happen at parties, I picked up her hand and I told her this was a new process to resolve phobias that used the meridian lines in the body and that I would tap on her at the endpoints of those meridians and that she should just repeat whatever I said. I tapped away on her; it worked beautifully.

Was this because I am an expert at EFT and have the ability to subtly establish rapport? Well, I like to think so, ☺ but no. It worked because I was lucky that it was an uncomplicated phobia and EFT works more often than not. Nothing wrong with "playing" with EFT occasionally. But it was a foolish thing to do. Not the least of which reason is that I could have spent my evening working on a complex phobia instead of enjoying my friends.

There are rare one-minute wonders in EFT. Less experienced practitioners may become lulled into thinking EFT will work every time with anything no matter how general. The process of resolving problem issues often takes great care and detective work. Most folks come to therapy with complex lives and complex issues and often with an attachment to keeping them. We can be very attached to our problems.

There is an American cowboy comedy with a classic line, *"Most problems,"* says the hero, *"don't amount to a hill of beans. But this is my hill, and these are my beans!"*

Working through those attachments to our hill and our beans can be challenging.

Carol Look, EFT Founding Master, wrote a series for the emofree.com website on the importance of *feeling safe to change*. She made several points about our fears:

- We fear the impact of the change on our life.
- We use our problems and conflicts to protect us from something.

- We are often ambivalent about change.
- We fear upsetting the balance in the relationships in our lives.
- We may be expected to do more if we change.
- We may change and still not be happy, and we have upset our world for nothing.

In other words, changes, even changes made easy with EFT, are scary. People's fears and issues are often deep and complex. At times we have a real challenge in addressing a deep issue. The competent EFTer becomes a detective, skilled at asking good questions and respecting the client's timing.

Back to the lady at my picnic with the spider phobia. Yes, it is fun to play with EFT, and important to preframe it as such when we do. Nothing wrong with a party trick or two from time to time. EFT is a seemingly simple but powerful therapeutic tool.

EFT can be simple; People can be powerfully complex.

My action was foolish because I didn't know anything about this person; I had no relationship. While I had tacit agreement to tap on her, she had not come to me for assistance with the spider phobia. For all I knew she could have been a complicated personality disorder or would abreact right in the middle of my picnic. She could have had her reasons to keep the attachment to her fear of spiders, maybe I was messing with the balance of her life. While she agreed when asked, she hadn't asked me to work with her and could have been "going along" because that was what was expected by the group but not what she wanted. I was lucky. It could have been much more complicated.

Besides, my action didn't fall under my definition of professionalism. I was not paying attention to the process of a relationship between two people. I was not getting out of my way. I was showing off. I was caught up in the game of the situation. I had an agenda. I was attached to the outcome. I was certainly not being congruent with my own beliefs of respect for the person. According to my beliefs, it was a very disrespectful thing to have done.

She did thank me later for resolving her spider phobia, and it all turned out OK. But it was not one of my crowning moments. I learned a valuable lesson that day.

> *Just having a successful EFT session does not excellence make!*

SEVENTH: Professionalism with a Capital "P"

Professionalism is a factor in excellence that is interwoven into everything we do.

We've looked at some of the traits of a professional. Professionals *get out of their way* and are *totally in the present.* They have an *in-depth knowledge of and respect* for the strengths of each client. They know the client has within themselves what they need to solve their problem. This belief makes it is easy for them to be *unattached to the outcome.*

But it is even more than that. A professional has confidence in his or her abilities because they have done the work it takes to achieve excellence. A professional is comfortable in his/her skin; they have clarity on who they are. They are congruent with actions and words.

Professionalism is shown in how you carry yourself, how you conduct yourself with people. It shows in your depth of knowledge in your response to questions. It particularly shows in how you respond to negative comments or criticism or demands on your time. It shows in how you treat people who have not yet reached your level of professionalism. It shows in your consideration for others while still respecting your boundaries.

It shows in your detective work and in your ability to get to the specifics in complex problems. It shows in your careful testing of the results.

It shows in your ability to use humor appropriately and respectfully.

I conducted an EFT session once with a young woman I had met on vacation, this time, with full permission and rapport established. This article, to the contrary, I rarely tap *on* people, but in this instance chose to do so. As we were working on her grief around the loss of her relationship, she apologized through her tears that her nose was running. I said, in a very deadpan voice, as I continued to tap, "No problem, I have hand sanitizer in the car." She laughed. Humor and laughter can be very healing and is a dynamite combination when used skillfully with EFT.

Excellence is wrapped up with professionalism. Professionalism is about:

- doing your work so you can be congruent with your actions and words.
- trusting the "process" of the relationship in the here and now between the two of you so you can fully understand your client.
- getting yourself out of the way so you can be in touch with your inner guidance.
- respecting people's ability to solve their problems so you can guide rather than lead.
- becoming unattached to the outcome so the client can fully explore their deepest world.

Making it look easy is the mark of a highly seasoned practitioner. Timing and a "right on" Setup *can* move a client to resolution quickly. How do you best learn that timing and right on statements? Well, partly through bad timing and wrong statements. Practice, practice, practice. Study, study, study. Excellence is not learned overnight.

NOTES

Do Not Push the River (It Flows by Itself) by Barry Stevens, 1970 Celestial Arts

About The Author

Ann Adams has almost 50 years as a clinical social worker—as a therapist, trainer, supervisor and administrator, 22 of those years included EFT. After learning about EFT in 1999, her goal became to help integrate this powerful tool effectively into helping professionals existing toolkit.

Ann is known for her ability to clearly explain concepts and make learning new skills fun. In this book, she shares an in-depth perspective and effective and efficient ways to utilize EFT to increase your results when working with others, with hints as well for using it more effectively for yourself.

This book helps all those who work with others in any capacity to better understand and deal with the complexities of people.

Ann's first formal EFT presentation was at Gary Craig's Specialty Series workshops in 2002, sharing her experience in working with children in a mental health setting and her administrative knowledge from experience in working in agencies on how to best introduce EFT to institutions.

She's since conducted EFT training and made multiple presentations about EFT at various professional and EFT conferences, workshops and events in the US, Canada, UK, Australia, and New Zealand.

Ann is now retired from certifications and licenses: LCSW,

ACEP-DCEP, ACP-CEP, EFT Honors, and the EFT International Trainer of Trainers. She was the director for the duration of Gary Craig's EFT Master Program. She organized five EFT Master Showcases in Boston, Dallas, Los Angeles, Denver, and Sydney, Australia. Those presentations are now available as a download on EFTMasterTraining.com. While she is "mostly" retired and no longer teaches certification classes she continues to write and teach introductory classes. From her broad and lengthy experience in the helping field and with EFT, she brings a broad perspective for working effectively with others.

EFT is Easy; People are Complex is not her first book. She's co-authored the set of *EFT Comprehensive Training Resource* [Level 1 and 2 and 3] books, which are used as a companion guide to EFT training classes. With her sister she wrote Sally and the Bully, a book for elementary school children about EFT. To help others share EFT more easily she also wrote the: *Insider's Guide to Planning and Creating a Successful Workshop* and the *Insider's Guide to Marketing Your EFT Practice*. In addition, she created *EFT4PowerPoint* training package taking much of the work out of planning an EFT workshop. This program, in its fourth upgrade, has literally been sold all over the world.

Ann lives in Rome, GA with her dog Morkie. She enjoys walking in the many wooded areas in NW Georgia and camping around the USA in a small camper van. Her main web site is www.AnnAdams.com.

www.ingramcontent.com/pod-product-compliance
Lightning Source LLC
Chambersburg PA
CBHW071702160426

43195CB00012B/1552